Practical Problems
for Managers

Practical
Problem Solving
for Managers

Michael Stevens

KOGAN
PAGE

BIM
BRITISH INSTITUTE OF MANAGEMENT

First published in 1988 by
Kogan Page Limited, 120 Pentonville Road, London N1 9JN,
in association with British Institute of Management

Photoset in North Wales by
Derek Doyle & Associates, Mold, Clwyd
Printed and bound in Great Britain

British Library Cataloguing in Publication Data

Stevens, Michael
    Practical problem solving for managers.
    1. Management. problem solving – Manuals
    I. Title   II. British Institute of
    Management
    658.4'03

    ISBN 1-85091-576-8

CONTENTS

How to use this book

Effective problem solving is a key management skill and a major factor in determining individual and organisational success. People with good problem solving skills adapt more quickly in times of rapid change and are generally the high achievers, whether it's by putting things right when they go wrong, making the best use of resources, or creating and exploiting opportunities.

Whatever your personal and professional ambitions, you can improve your chances of achieving what you want by developing your problem solving skills.

Each of us has an innate ability to solve problems. To develop this ability you need a clear understanding of the skills and techniques involved and practise in applying them in different situations. Throughout this book you will see the following symbols:

 ## ACTIVITIES

for you to do, which help to improve your understanding of problem solving and practise the skills and techniques involved.

 ## GUIDELINES

providing feedback on your work on the Activities.

PROJECTS

at the end of the chapters, giving you the opportunity to summarise and apply what you have learnt.

KEY
POINTS

to remember, as a summary of each chapter.

Practice is an essential element in learning how to solve problems effectively and occasionally you will find it useful to have a large notepad to write down your ideas.

The book is divided into 12 chapters which help you to learn step-by-step to improve your problem solving skills. Although you can read the chapters in any order, since the basis of good problem solving is a methodical approach, you will benefit most by working through them in sequence.

This book has been written for everyone who wants the success, recognition and peace of mind which can be achieved through effective problem solving.

Introduction

In its broadest sense, problem solving consists of devising a course of action which will enable you to achieve a particular goal or objective. It plays a fundamental role in our day-to-day lives, both through our own actions and those of others which affect us. Solving problems effectively requires an understanding of the problem solving process and the ability to use the appropriate skills and techniques at the right time.

Success or failure?

Whether you are trying to achieve something specific, such as locating and correcting a fault, or looking at broader issues, such as how to improve your efficiency at work, the way you tackle a problem can mean the difference between success and failure.

An American airline was trying to improve seat occupancy on one of its loss-making routes. After reducing the fare one of its competitors undercut it. The airline had a choice to make: should it reduce the fare even further; cease flights on that route and withdraw from the competition; or was there another solution?

In fact, the airline chose to run a promotional campaign. It offered to match the competitor's lower fare, although anyone paying the regular fare would receive a free bottle of whisky.

This was an effective solution. The airline was able to buy the whisky at a reduced price, so the actual cost of the promotion was lower than the added value perceived by the customer. In addition, the route was popular with businessmen and having their company pay for their whisky was very attractive!

An outbreak of salmonella poisoning was linked by Department of Health investigations to one of a company's four food products. The company immediately closed its factory for a thorough investigation, but was unable to trace the source of the contamination.

Two days later more cases were reported. Further investigation at the manufacturing plant had still failed to pinpoint the problem. Believing that it was impossible for this to happen again, the company announced that all existing stocks of the product would be destroyed.

Media coverage of these events had raised public concern and severely damaged the company's image. Sales of its four products fell sharply. Financially weakened, the company became the target of a successful takeover bid.

Unlike the airline, the food manufacturer was unable to solve its problem, with serious consequences. Firstly, it failed to locate the source of the salmonella contamination or to suggest how it might have happened. Secondly, it was unable to restore public confidence that it could not happen again.

Many of the reasons why people do not find effective solutions to their problems can be grouped under three headings:

- they are not methodical
- they lack knowledge of the techniques available to help in solving problems, or are unable to use them effectively
- they use methods inappropriate to the particular problem.

How this book will help

Using a systematic approach increases your chances of solving problems effectively. To be a good problem solver you need to understand what the various stages of problem solving involve and learn how to apply the appropriate skills and techniques. This book will help you to:

- understand **what is involved in solving problems** (Chapter 1)
- analyse **how you currently tackle problems** (Chapter 2)
- **recognise and overcome barriers** to finding good solutions (Chapter 3)
- understand **how your working environment can affect the quality of your solutions**, and learn how to ensure that it doesn't have a detrimental effect (Chapter 4)
- improve your ability to **recognise and define problems** (Chapter 5)
- use **appropriate strategies** for finding a solution (Chapter 6)
- use appropriate **models to represent problems** and specific **idea generation techniques** (Chapter 7)
- **work in a group** to solve problems (Chapter 8)
- **evaluate solutions** to select the best available (Chapter 9)
- **get solutions accepted** (Chapter 10)
- **implement solutions** effectively (Chapter 11), and
- create **an Action Plan** which you can use as a guide for solving problems in the future (Chapter 12).

The first step in developing your problem solving skills is to understand clearly what problems are and how they are solved. This is the subject of Chapter 1.

Chapter 1

Problems and how we solve them

What are problems?

We use the word problem to describe *a wide range of situations of different importance* , from the irritation of discovering that the car battery is flat, to the life threatening failure of an aircraft engine in mid-air.

 ACTIVITY

Think about the things which have been and are currently a 'problem' for you and try to answer the following questions.

How would you define the word 'problem'?

How do problems arise?

What does problem solving achieve?

GUIDELINES

Problems can be defined broadly as *situations in which we experience uncertainty or difficulty in achieving what we want to achieve*, eg

- Stopping smoking is a problem when you decide you want to stop but cannot.
- A computer malfunction is a problem if it prevents you completing work on time.
- An excessive workload is a problem when it interferes with your ability to work effectively.
- Poor communication is a problem when it reduces the efficiency of an organisation.

Problems arise when an obstacle prevents us reaching an objective, eg when a breakdown in a company's manufacturing plant (the obstacle) prevents it fulfilling orders (the objective).

Objective = something we have decided we need to achieve.

Obstacle = anything that prevents us achieving an objective.

---

objective + obstacle = PROBLEM

We encounter a large variety of problems during the course of our work, with objectives and obstacles of different types and importance. *Defining these accurately is essential to finding an effective solution.*

Our perspective on problems can also change. For example, after his advertising and promotions budget had been cut, the marketing director of a tobacco company had to find ways of maintaining the same high profile for the company's brands. However, this was completely overshadowed days later when the Government announced extensive new restrictions on cigarette advertising.

The objectives involved may not always be our own. Sometimes we become involved in *solving problems which are not our direct responsibility*. In these situations it's important to identify the 'owner' of the problem.

Problem solving can be used to achieve more than simply putting things right when they go wrong. Since a problem exists when an obstacle prevents us achieving an objective, problem solving can help us to achieve objectives we set ourselves. This means that *we can use problem solving to create and exploit opportunities*.

If everything is running smoothly it's natural to assume that there are no problems to be tackled. This is a dangerous mistake, even for people currently leading their field. If they fail to change and develop, while others are moving ahead, they will inevitably fall behind the competition. In a market-led economy originality and innovation are vital to success. **Problem solving can and should be used in any situation where there is potential for improvement** .

Problems can be divided broadly into two groups:

- those where the current situation is not what was expected (known as **closed** or **maintenance problems**)
- those where we want to change our current situation in some way but there is an obstacle preventing us doing so (known as **open-ended** or **achievement problems**).

Closed problems occur when something has happened that should not have happened, or something we expected to happen has not happened, ie there is a deviation from the normal or expected state of affairs. For example, it could be the unexpected resignation of a key member of staff, or the failure of the principal speaker to arrive at a conference. The cause (or obstacle) may be known or unknown, but something needs to be done about it.

Open-ended problems occur when we want to achieve a specific objective but there are certain obstacles blocking our progress. They can be subdivided into three groups:

- where we are unable to reach our current objective, eg failing to meet a sales target
- where our current objective could be exceeded, eg improved efficiency
- where a new objective could be achieved through problem solving, eg creating a new product or service.

Solving a problem involves finding ways to overcome any obstacles and to achieve our objective. This book concentrates on the mental skills and processes involved although others, such as interpersonal and manual skills, may be required.

Although each problem is unique in terms of the information involved, and requires a unique blend of thought processes to find a solution, all successful problem solving follows a basic pattern.

The stages of problem solving

The problem solving process can be divided in different ways and the stages have been given various labels. This has been done to make it easier to understand but how it is divided and the labels that are used are not important. To be a successful problem solver *you need to understand what the stages involve and follow them methodically* whenever you encounter a problem.

ACTIVITY

Think about the most recent occasions on which you have had to solve a problem. Try to recall the stages you went through and list them below.

GUIDELINES

To be a successful problem solver you must go through these stages:

- recognising and defining the problem
- finding possible solutions
- choosing the best solution
- implementing the solution.

These stages are examined in detail in subsequent chapters, but here is a summary of what is involved at each stage.

1.   Recognising and defining the problem

Obviously, before any action can be taken to solve a problem, you need to **recognise that a problem exists**. A surprising number of problems go unnoticed or are only recognised when the situation becomes serious. Opportunities are also missed. There are specific techniques you can use to help you recognise problems and opportunities.

Once you have recognised a problem you need to give it a label – a tentative definition. This serves to focus your search for relevant information, from which you can write an accurate description or **definition** of the problem.

The process of definition differs for closed and open-ended problems. With closed problems you need to define all the circumstances surrounding the deviation from the norm. Sometimes this will provide strong clues as to the cause of the problem. Defining open-ended problems involves identifying and defining your objectives and any obstacles which could prevent you reaching them. The problem definition provides the basis for finding solutions.

2.   Finding possible solutions

Closed problems generally have one or a limited number of possible solutions, while open-ended problems usually can be solved in a large number of ways. The most effective solution to an open-ended problem is found by selecting the best from a wide range of possibilities. Finding solutions involves analysing the problem to ensure that you fully understand it and then constructing courses of action which will achieve your objective.

Analysing the problem involves identifying and collecting the relevant information and representing it in a meaningful way. Analysing closed problems helps you to identify all the possible causes and confirm the real cause, or obstacle, before looking for a solution. With open-ended problems you are looking for information which will help to suggest a range of possible ways to solve the problem. Analysis also helps you to decide what the ideal solution would be, which helps to guide your search for solutions.

Constructing courses of action to solve the problem involves discovering what actions will deal with any obstacles and achieve your objective. Workable solutions are developed by combining and modifying ideas and a range of creative techniques are available to help in this process. The more ideas you have to work with, the better your chances of finding an effective solution.

3.   Choosing the best solution

This is the stage at which you *evaluate the possible solutions* and select that which will be most effective in solving the problem. It's a process of decision making based on a comparison of the potential outcome of alternative solutions. This involves

- identifying all the features of an ideal solution, including the constraints it has to meet
- eliminating solutions which do not meet the constraints

- evaluating the remaining solutions against the outcome required
- assessing the risks associated with the 'best' solution
- making the decision to implement this solution

A problem is only solved when a solution has been implemented. In some situations, before this can take place, you need to *gain acceptance of the solution by other people*, or get their authority to implement it. This may involve various strategies of persuasion.

4. Implementing the solution

This involves three separate stages:

- planning and preparing to implement the solution
- taking the appropriate action and monitoring its effects
- reviewing the ultimate success of the action

Implementing your solution is the culmination of all your efforts and requires **very careful planning**. The plan describes the sequence of actions required to achieve the objective, the timescale and the resources required at each stage. Ways of minimising the risks involved and preventing mistakes have to be devised and built into the plan. Details of what must be done if things go wrong are also included.

Once the plan has been put into effect, the situation has to be monitored to ensure that things are running smoothly. Any problems or potential problems have to be dealt with quickly. When the action is completed it's necessary to measure its success, both to estimate its usefulness for solving future problems of this type and to ensure that the problem has been solved. If not, further action may be required.

These stages provide *a very flexible framework which can be adapted to suit all problems*. With closed problems, for example, where there is likely to be only one or a few solutions, the emphasis will be on defining and analysing the problem to indicate possible causes. Open-ended problems, on the other hand, require more work at the idea generation stage to develop a large range of possible solutions.

At any stage in solving a problem it may be necessary to go back and adapt work done at an earlier stage. A variety of techniques and strategies are available to help you at each stage and these are described in later chapters.

The following outline shows how these stages lead to the solution of a problem.

Stage of problem solving	Example
Recognising the problem	— Sales analysis has shown a fall in sales in the North East
Defining the problem: Current situation	— Sales in the North East have fallen by 10% in the past month
Desired situation	— Sales in the North East restored to previous level at least
Objective	— Restore sales in the North East to previous level within 3 months
Analysing the problem	— Salesman for North East is John Davies — Davies moved home 3 weeks ago — New home is in South Wales — Travelling time to sales area is 3 hours — Davies' sales day starts at 10am and ends at 3.30pm
Possible solutions	— Replace Davies in North East — Offer Davies cash incentive to spend weekdays in North East — Restructure sales areas
Criteria for an ideal solution	— No extra cost — Keep Davies in North East if possible, for his experience
Best solution	— Replace Davies
Implementing the solution	— John Davies offered alternative employment — New salesman for North East recruited and trained
Reviewing success	— John Davies resigns — Sales in North East up by 15% within 3 weeks

The different stages of problem solving involve manipulating information in various ways and require different mental skills.

The skills of problem solving

Problem solving requires two distinct types of mental skill, analytical and creative.

Analytical or logical thinking includes skills such as ordering, comparing, contrasting, evaluating and selecting. It provides a logical framework for problem solving and helps to select the best alternative from those available by narrowing down the range of possibilities (a **convergent** process). Analytical thinking often predominates in solving closed problems, where the many possible causes have to be identified and analysed to find the real cause.

Creative thinking is a **divergent** process, using the imagination to create a large range of ideas for solutions. It requires us to look beyond the obvious, creating ideas which may, at first, seem unrealistic or have no logical connection with the problem. There is a large element of creative thinking in solving open problems.

The creative thinking skills can be divided into several key elements:

- fluency   – producing many ideas
- flexibility   – producing a broad range of ideas
- originality   – producing uncommon ideas
- elaboration – developing ideas.

Effective problem solving requires a controlled mixture of analytical and creative thinking.

Research has shown that, in general terms, each side or hemisphere of the brain is specialised to serve one of these groups of skills. The degree of specialisation of each hemisphere varies from person to person, but it has given rise to the terms right-brain thinking and left-brain thinking. **Left-brain thinking** is more logical and analytical, and is predominantly verbal. **Right-brain thinking** is more holistic and is concerned with feelings and impressionistic relationships.

To be a good problem solver you need to be able to switch from one group of skills to the other and back again, although this is not always easy. Traditional education gives far greater encouragement to the development and use of left-brain thinking. This is reinforced in the way we are required to work, where emphasis is placed on rational, logical analysis of data in drawing conclusions. The idea generation techniques discussed in Chapters 7 and 8 are designed to help you to overcome these restraints.

Some other terms which are often used in discussions of creativity include:

Intuition – the ability to draw conclusions based on impressions and feelings rather than hard facts. It is a characteristic of right-brain thinking and some people rely on it more than others.

Incubation – the period between stopping conscious work on a problem and the time when we become aware of a solution or part solution. People struggling with problems often suddenly become aware of a solution after a period of incubation, during which the mind is occupied by other things.

Invention – the creation of new, meaningful ideas or concepts.

Innovation – putting new ideas or concepts to a practical use, as in the development of a new product or service.

Why people fail to solve problems effectively

Solving problems is a complex process and each of us is better at the skills required at some stages than others.

ACTIVITY

Make a list of the reasons why you think people may not find the best solutions to their problems. Many of them have been hinted at in this chapter.

GUIDELINES

Your list may have included others as well, but some of the reasons why people fail to find effective solutions include

- not being methodical
- lack of commitment to solving the problem
- misinterpreting the problem
- lack of knowledge of the techniques and processes involved in problem solving
- inability to use the techniques effectively
- using a method inappropriate to the particular problem
- insufficient or inaccurate information
- inability to combine analytical and creative thinking
- failure to ensure effective implementation.

Chapter 2 will help you to assess your own approach to problem solving.

KEY POINTS

- A problem exists when an obstacle prevents you reaching an objective.
- Problem solving can be divided into stages, which you must follow methodically if you want to be sure of finding an effective solution.
- Solving problems effectively requires a controlled mixture of analytical and creative thinking skills.

PROJECT

Select a problem that you are currently facing and write an outline plan of the steps you will take to solve it eg a definition of the problem and what information you will require.

How do you tackle problems?

One of the best ways to learn or to improve a skill is to receive coaching from a teacher. This provides you with guidance on your current ability and appropriate practice to build on your strengths and overcome your weaknesses. This chapter is designed to help you assess your current approach to solving problems – your strengths and your weaknesses. It takes the form of four brief questionnaires devoted to subjects covered in subsequent chapters.

 ACTIVITY

Tick the statements which apply to you. Be honest.

Section A

1 I try to avoid situations which involve taking risks.

2 I feel uncomfortable in new situations.

3 I always try to take the quickest route in finishing a task.

4 I think it's important always to do the 'right' thing.

5 I'm sometimes too quick in jumping to conclusions.

6 I dislike having to ask for advice.

7 When I think I'm right I stick to my guns no matter what.

8 I'm wary of suggesting new ideas at work because I know I won't get much encouragement or support.

9 Sometimes I find it difficult to make people understand my ideas.

10 I am happier in an environment where everyone sticks to the rules.

11 It's competitive at work and I'm aware that I have to defend my position.

12 I would feel embarrassed suggesting unusual or impractical ideas in a meeting.

13 I get frustrated with situations that aren't clear-cut.

14 Sometimes I feel that I don't receive due credit for my ideas.

15 I don't like people to question my decisions.

16 Once I've made up my mind usually nothing will change it.

17 I tend to be cautious in the ideas that I express to my more senior colleagues.

18 If I've found a method that works well I stick with it.

19 I probably couldn't explain to someone exactly how I solve problems.

20 At work I'm not encouraged to improve my performance.

Give yourself one point for each statement you ticked and write down the total:

Section B

I make sure I know all the facts before I make a decision. (6)

I don't go looking for problems. (2)

I often review how well I've achieved what I set out to do. (5)

I tend to jump in and do things rather than thinking about them much first. (1)

I usually plan carefully how I'm going to do something before I begin. (6)

When I've finished one job I like to get on with the next one without looking back. (2)

I assess the consequences before I take any action. (5)

When I have a problem which involves other people I like to have found a solution before discussing it with them. (3)

When I need to get other people's agreement to an idea I think about how I can make it sound attractive to them. (4)

I find planning boring and keep it to a minimum. (2)

I'm always prepared for potential problems. (6)

To find out if something will work I prefer to try it rather than analysing it. (1)

When I have a problem which involves other people I like to discuss it with them before looking for a solution. (4)

Usually I make decisions quickly without much deliberation. (1)

I like to tackle things step-by-step. (5)

Sometimes I have jumped to conclusions which turned out to be wrong. (1)

If someone questions a decision I've made usually I can explain to them exactly why. (5)

I try to exert pressure on people when I need their agreement. (2)

When I have to do something new I feel more confident following a plan. (4)

I would find it difficult to explain to other people my reasons for making particular decisions. (2)

Add up the numbers given at the end of each statement you ticked and write down your score:

Section C

1. I understand situations best by analysing them carefully.

2. I tend to believe in ideas more when they 'feel' right.

3. I think I'm a very practical, down-to-earth sort of person.

4. When discussing ideas I tend to support the people who show the strongest conviction.

5. I tend to judge ideas by how practical they sound.

6. I enjoy meticulous research.

7. When I'm listening to ideas I tend to support those which are backed up by hard facts.

8. I understand complex situations best by trying to picture them in my mind.

9. If things are not working out as I expected I make every effort to find out why.

10. I like dreaming up unusual ways to do things.

11. I feel more confident making a decision when I can weigh up all the facts first.

12. As soon as I come across a problem my mind races with ideas about it.

13. I think first impressions often turn out to be right.

14. I often catch myself daydreaming about how I would like things to be.

15. I place a high value on people being logical.

16. In meetings I make sure that any ideas I suggest are practical and relevant.

17. I tend to look at situations as a whole rather than breaking them down into separate parts.

18. In meetings usually I come up with unusual ways to tackle situations.

19. I think analysis and planning take all the fun out of things and try to avoid them.

20. I feel more comfortable when things are very orderly.

21. I often try to visualise problems.

22. I would never act on a hunch alone.

Section D

I often question why things are done in a particular way. (5)

I am content with my current situation. (2)

I like to remain in the background and just get on with my job. (1)

I often experiment with new ways to do things. (6)

I like to receive recognition for my ideas. (5)

I like to have established routines to follow. (2)

I sometimes get bored with my work and feel that I don't always give it my best. (2)

I regularly set myself new targets to achieve. (5)

At the end of the day I switch off from work completely. (1)

I spend a lot of time thinking about and planning how I could achieve what I want in life. (6)

I often do things because they are politic, rather than because I believe in them. (1)

I get unsettled when things change significantly. (2)

I get a kick out of helping people to solve their problems. (5)

I prefer to get on with my work rather than wasting time trying to change the way things are done. (1)

I tend to lose heart and give up when things don't go as planned. (1)

I often get ideas about work problems when I'm not at work. (5)

I don't like to get involved in other people's problems. (1)

I often spend time dreaming up ways to improve the things around me. (6)

I enjoy a challenge. (5)

When I get an idea usually I'm determined to follow it through. (5)
I prefer to take life as it comes rather than looking ahead. (1)

Add up the numbers given at the end of each statement you ticked and write down your score:

GUIDELINES

Most of us are better at certain aspects of problem solving than others. We have different abilities in the various skills required and different attitudes to tackling problems. Your scores in these questionnaires should give you a broad idea of how you tackle problems.

Section A

These questions relate to some of the factors which can hinder problem solving. The higher your score out of 20 the more likely you are to be hindered by them. Chapter 3 examines these factors in detail and tells you how you can improve your problem solving by overcoming them.

Section B

These questions were designed to assess how methodical you are in solving problems. The lower your score the less methodical you are likely to be in your approach. A score of **under 25** suggests that you could make much better use of your skills simply by learning to be more methodical. If you scored **25–39** you are probably not methodical at all stages of the problem solving process. For scores of **40 or over** give yourself a pat on the back, but don't be complacent. Practice is the only way to stay on top. Being methodical is essential in solving problems effectively.

Section C

This section helped to assess whether you have a bias towards analytical or creative thinking. Transfer your answers to the question numbers listed below. Give yourself one point for each question you ticked and add up the total in each column.

2

	1
4	3
8	5
10	6
12	7
13	9
14	11
17	15
18	16
19	20
21	22

creative	analytical
thinking	thinking

A difference in score between the two columns suggests that you have a natural bias towards the higher scoring type of thinking. The larger the difference, the stronger the bias.

An **analytical bias** means that you prefer the logical approach, investigating problems carefully to find all the relevant facts and to ensure that you fully understand the situation. At times this may lead you to overlook novel ideas which are not directly related to the problem but which could lead to good solutions. You could benefit from practice in applying your creative thinking skills at the appropriate stages of problem solving.

A **creative bias** means that you prefer to use your imagination and intuition to help you understand problems and to draw conclusions about what action is required to solve them. At times you may fail to gain all the relevant information and not understand the true nature of a problem and its implications. You could benefit from learning to be more analytical at the appropriate stages of problem solving.

Effective problem solving requires a controlled mixture of analytical and creative thinking. A good problem solver knows how and at which stage to apply creative and analytical skills.

Section D

This section relates to your general attitude towards problems and problem solving. The higher your score the more active you are in applying your problem solving skills. A score of **45 or over** suggests that you have a natural enthusiasm for seeking out and solving problems and have a certain degree of confidence in your problem solving skills. A score of **25 or less** suggests that you would prefer to avoid problems, perhaps because you lack confidence in being able to solve them effectively or because you are not aware of the benefits resulting from solving problems effectively.

An enthusiasm for problem solving can't be learnt directly but it can be developed. The more practice you have in solving problems the easier it becomes and the more you recognise the benefits it brings.

This chapter should have helped you to recognise some of your strengths and weaknesses. The remaining chapters of the book will help you to learn techniques and strategies to help you overcome your weaknesses and build on your strengths.

KEY
POINTS

- To improve your skill in solving problems first you need to recognise your strengths and weaknesses.
- Practice is the best way to build on your strengths and overcome your weaknesses.
- There are various strategies and techniques you can learn to improve your skill in solving problems.

PROJECT

Look through your scores on the Activity and list your
strengths and weaknesses.

My strengths	**My weaknesses**

After reading this book you may find it useful to read through this chapter again to see if you think your approach is going to change in the light of what you have learnt.

Chapter 3

Barriers to finding the best solution

Some of the reasons we do not find the most effective solutions to our problems have been mentioned already. This chapter looks in detail at a range of factors known as **'blocks'** which can hinder your problem solving. It will help you to learn to recognise and overcome them.

What are problem solving blocks?

A block is *anything which prevents us finding an effective solution to a problem*. We all experience them, but of different types and intensities. The blocks have been grouped in various ways by different authors according to their cause, eg

Problem solving strategies	Knowledge and fluency in the language of the problem
Values	Perception
Perception	Cultural and social effects
Self-image	Emotional or personal factors

The way the blocks are classified is not of great importance because there is considerable overlap between groups. This chapter uses a popular classification which divides the blocks into six categories:

- perceptual
- emotional
- intellectual
- expressive
- environmental
- cultural

It's important that you are able to recognise when blocks are hindering your problem solving so that you can take action to overcome them.

What causes these blocks?

The labels applied to these blocks give some clues to their origins.

Perceptual blocks arise from the way we have learnt to recognise information from the world around us. We develop habits of 'seeing' the world, which sometimes can get in the way of finding the best solution to a problem, eg seeing only the most obvious solution.

Emotional blocks arise when our emotional needs conflict with the situation, eg when we do not propose a radical solution to a problem because we feel it might sound ridiculous and make us look foolish.

Intellectual blocks are caused by us not being able to assimilate information in the ways required to solve a problem, eg not knowing how to evaluate ideas to select the most effective solution.

Expressive blocks arise when we are unable to communicate in the way required to produce an effective solution, eg not being able to express our ideas effectively to those who have to implement the solution.

Environmental blocks are caused by external obstacles in the social or physical environment, which prevent us from solving a problem effectively, eg distractions from the task.

Cultural blocks result from our conditioning to accept what is expected or 'normal' in a given situation, eg when the work ethic says that we must be serious-minded, but finding an effective solution requires some playful fantasy.

All of the blocks, except those caused by the physical environment, arise through learning or lack of it, either our own or that of people who influence us. For example:

If you have never learnt a draughtsman's skills, or to use computer aided design, you may find it difficult to provide drawings for the manufacture of a new component you have visualised (an expressive block).

If your colleagues have learnt that competition is the route to success and you suggest to them ideas which put you ahead in the race, those ideas are likely to be ignored, strongly criticised or suppressed (an environmental block).

We can overcome most of our own blocks permanently by re-learning, and overcome other people's blocks which hinder us by learning ways to sidestep them.

Recognising problem solving blocks

The first step in overcoming blocks is to find out which blocks affect you, both directly and through other people.

 ACTIVITY

List two ways in which each of the following factors could hinder your problem solving.

A. The complexity of a problem which has many interrelated facets.

B. Your feelings about a problem situation and its possible solutions.

C. Your thinking skills.

GUIDELINES

Each of these factors relates to one of the groups of blocks identified earlier. There is a great variety of blocks within each group and you may recognise some of those you have listed amongst the following descriptions.

A. Perceptual blocks

Perceptual blocks exist when we are unable to clearly perceive a problem or the information needed to solve it effectively. They include:

Seeing only what you expect to see
To recognise situations we look for patterns of key features which we have learnt by experience represent a particular situation. If the key features 'fit' we assume the situations are the same. This often obscures the true nature of a problem, either because we exclude relevant information (because it isn't a key feature or didn't occur in the past), or include information simply because we assume it is there.

Stereotyping
In recognising situations we automatically apply labels (like door, machine, laziness) which can prevent us seeing all the features of the situation. Often we don't look beyond the obvious. For example, if someone isn't working as hard as we would like and we apply the label 'lazy' to that person, we might overlook the possibility that boredom with monotonous work is the problem, and not laziness.

Not recognising problems
A surprising number of problems go unnoticed or are recognised only when the effects have become severe and emergency action is required.

Not seeing the problem in perspective

This is related to some of the previous blocks, and results from:

- taking too narrow a view of the situation, so that we recognise only part of the problem or the information required to solve it
- failing to recognise how different parts of the problem are related
- seeing only superficial aspects of the problem, so that the solution is inadequate
- failing to see the problem from the point of view of other people who are involved.

Mistaking cause and effect

Many problems are recognised by their effects or the absence of expected results. If cause and effect are confused then we are unlikely to find an effective solution. For example, if goods do not arrive and we assume that the supplier is late in despatching them when in fact our ordering department has failed to send out the order, then our search for solutions will be misdirected. In this situation the late despatch of the goods is an effect of the problem and not a cause.

B. Emotional blocks

Emotional blocks exist when we perceive a threat to our emotional needs. These needs differ in type and strength from person to person but include needs for achievement, recognition, order, belonging and self-esteem. The emotional blocks include:

Fear of making mistakes or looking foolish

This is the most significant emotional block because it affects most of us and is difficult to overcome. As a result of traditional schooling, the expected reaction when we make a mistake or suggest radically different ideas is laughter and ridicule. No one likes being laughed at and as a result we learn to fear making mistakes and to avoid suggesting ideas which are different.

This block becomes more severe in the presence of colleagues of a different rank to our own. With those who are more
senior we imagine that we will be thought inexperienced or
immature. With those more junior we want to protect our
image as being knowledgeable and experienced.

Impatience

Being impatient to solve a problem may be due either to a
desire to succeed quickly or to end the discomfort or loss
caused by the problem. This has two major consequences.
We tend to grab the first solution which comes along,
without adequate analysis of the problem, and we evaluate
ideas too fast, almost instinctively rejecting unusual ideas.
Either way, our solution is unlikely to be the most effective
available.

Avoiding anxiety

This is another common block. Some of us are more
susceptible to anxiety and also find it more unpleasant than
others. Many factors can cause anxiety, including high risk,
disorder and ambiguity, long-term stress, and fear for our
security. The effects on problem solving include avoiding
risks, indecision in situations which are not 'black and
white', excessive reliance on others' judgement, and
avoiding challenging the status quo.

Fear of taking risks

This leads to the avoidance of situations where the outcome
is uncertain or could be unpleasant. A major cause is our
desire for security. The consequences include setting
objectives within easy reach, so that there is no risk of
failure, and accepting known solutions in preference to the
unusual because their value is certain. A liking for taking
risks and over-confidence in being able to avoid unpleasant
consequences are more dangerous blocks.

Need for order

This is related to avoiding anxiety. It can lead to an inability to cope with the frustration of situations which are not clear cut or where ambiguities exist.

Lack of challenge

This may arise when the problem is routine or the benefits/losses are not significant to us. The result is that either we don't tackle the problem or we take the easiest, quickest route to solution.

C. Intellectual blocks

Intellectual blocks exist when we don't have the necessary thinking skills to find a successful solution, or are unable to use them effectively. They include:

Lack of knowledge or skill in the problem solving process

This is one of the most common blocks. It includes: inadequate skills in analytical and creative thinking; an inflexible strategy, using one approach for every type of problem; the inability to use the various problem solving techniques. They can all lead to ineffective solutions.

Lack of creative thinking

This is always caused by an inability to use the skills rather than their absence, resulting from the dominance of analytical thinking in our day-to-day lives and a lack of practice.

Inflexible thinking

This is a difficulty in switching from one type of thinking skill to another, such as from analysis to idea generation or from verbal to visual thinking.

Not being methodical

This is perhaps the most common block. A step-by-step approach is essential to solving problems effectively.

Lack of knowledge or skill in using the 'language' of the problem

If a problem involves a language that we cannot understand or cannot use, such as specialist jargon or statistical analysis, we will not be able to tackle the problem effectively. Similarly, we may use an inappropriate language, such as trying to find an error in accounts by describing the situation verbally rather than analysing it mathematically.

Using inadequate information

This happens when we do not make sufficient effort to collect the relevant information, or do not understand what information is relevant, where to find it, or how it relates to the problem. Similarly, using inaccurate information can lead us to the wrong conclusions.

ACTIVITY

The following factors relate to the remaining three groups of blocks. List two ways in which each one could hinder your problem solving.

D. Your ability to express and explain ideas.

E. The place that you work – the rules and regulations, the people and surroundings.

F. What is generally expected, or accepted as good or right in a particular situation.

GUIDELINES

You may recognise some of your ideas amongst the following.

D. Expressive blocks

Expressive blocks exist when we do not have the knowledge or skills necessary to communicate or record ideas in the ways required. They are caused by an inability to use 'languages' effectively, such as words, drawings, mathematics, scientific symbols, and so on. They include:

Using the wrong language
Some problems are more effectively solved or communicated using one language rather than another. For example, we are unlikely to get very far if we record data only verbally when the problem requires quantitative analysis. Similarly, people may find it hard to grasp our meaning if we try to explain our feelings about a situation using mathematics instead of words.

Unfamiliarity with a particular application of a language
The most obvious example is the difficulty many people have making a speech, even though they can write their ideas effectively on paper.

Inadequate explanations
These can result from a real lack of information about what you are trying to convey, or from assuming that your audience already has some of the information when they don't.

A passive management style
A situation where we are reluctant to or find it difficult to

exert influence may prevent us communicating our ideas effectively. This is particularly important when people need to be convinced of the validity of ideas.

A dominant management style

This is when we exert oppressive control, either deliberately or unconsciously, and can make those we are communicating with automatically reluctant to accept what we say or hostile to our ideas.

E. Environmental blocks

Environmental blocks, which exist when the social or physical environment hinders our problem solving, are examined in detail in Chapter 4, but they include:

Management style

The way in which we are managed can influence both our attitude to problem solving and the freedom we have to create and implement ideas. For example, if our ideas are dismissed constantly with comments such as 'No, it wouldn't work because ...', or 'No, we've tried it before and it didn't work', we soon give up trying.

Distractions

Due to excessive noise and interruptions, these affect some people more than others, but in general they have a detrimental effect on problem solving.

Physical discomfort

This can create a distraction as well as resulting in stress or lethargy depending on the circumstances. For example, poorly designed chairs may create a distraction by giving us backache which, in turn, can make us irritable and less interested in any type of work.

Lack of support

This comes in many forms. For example, we may need specialist information, advice, skills or other resources, or authority to take action. A more pervasive aspect of this block is a lack of encouragement and the necessary organisational structure to support and exploit people's ideas.

Stress
Stress due to pressure of work and deadlines, affects people differently. For those who are susceptible to stress it can be a powerful block, hindering creative thinking in particular.

Lack of communication
This has a number of effects, including inability to get the information you require and a lack of encouragement.

Monotonous work
This can dull enthusiasm for solving problems and put us onto 'automatic pilot', making us blind to problems when they occur.

Expectations of others
These can influence both our general performance in problem solving and the objectives we set ourselves. For example, if our peers and superiors are happy with a regular solution to a problem we may feel that it's a waste of time looking for a new, more effective solution. On the other hand, if we are expected to find an innovative solution we are likely to make a greater effort.

F. Cultural blocks

Cultural blocks exist when our problem solving is hindered by accepting that some things are good or right and are done, while others are bad or wrong and are not done, so that we become bound by custom. They include:

Unquestioning acceptance of the status quo
There is a tendency to conform to established ideas and methods of working and not to question them or express ideas which depart from them. If something is not normally

done we tend to look for the reasons why it can't be done or why it wouldn't work, rather than looking for the reasons why it should be done or why it could work.

Dislike of change

The attitude that tradition is preferable to change can arise from the need for security. If a situation is acceptable as it is, any change, which must involve some uncertainty, is felt to be threatening by some people. However, as we become more and more accustomed to change this block is becoming less common, but there must be reasons for change. Change for change's sake can be dangerous.

Fantasy and humour are not productive

There is still a widespread belief that fantasy and humour have no place in the serious business of problem solving. Subjective reports from innovators suggest otherwise. Fantasy and humour are connected by one common feature – the unlikely combination of ideas (think about it next time you hear a good joke – the punch line is always unexpected). Innovative solutions to problems arise in the same way – by making a link between apparently unrelated ideas.

Feelings, intuition and subjective judgements are unreliable

There is a strong bias towards reason, logic and quantitative judgements because they can be measured and communicated in accurate terms. Feelings, intuition and subjective judgements, which cannot be measured or communicated as effectively, are seen as unrealiable and are mistrusted.

Even in mathematics, one of the most logical of sciences, intuition is often reported as playing a key role in problem solving. A good problem solver needs to be able to use both objective, logical methods and subjective, intuitive methods in the search for solutions.

Over-emphasis on competition or cooperation

A strongly competitive environment (for recognition, promotion, and so on) can make people unwilling to listen to the ideas of those with whom they are competing. Similarly, in a strongly cooperative environment we may avoid expressing new ideas because we don't want to stand out from the crowd.

Taboos

Some actions and ideas are excluded from problem solving because they are regarded as distasteful, or are harmful, or contravene accepted moral codes. For example, in a test of creativity a group of students were given a problem to solve using calculus. They had to follow certain rules and the objective was to see who produced the largest number of different routes to the correct solution. A few students produced a lot more than the others because they chose to break the rules they were told to follow.

Although eventually we may not decide to break a taboo, there is no harm in breaking them in thought. This can often lead to new perspectives on a problem.

The labels given to all of these blocks only serve to help explain them. There is considerable overlap between some of the blocks and this can make it hard to recognise them if you look for labels. **The most effective way to recognise blocks** is to examine your thinking when you are solving problems and be aware constantly for factors which are hindering your progress.

Overcoming problem solving blocks

Because they arise in different ways, the various blocks require different techniques to overcome them.

ACTIVITY

Briefly describe how you think you could achieve the following.

Ensure that you fully understand a problem.

Overcome the fear of looking foolish.

Overcome a dislike for taking risks.

Ensure that you choose the best method for solving a particular problem.

Explain your ideas effectively.

Avoid distractions when you are working on a problem.

Not be misled into thinking things couldn't be improved.

GUIDELINES

These questions relate to only some of the blocks covered in this chapter. You may recognise your suggestions for overcoming them amongst the following methods:

Perceptual blocks

These are relatively easy to overcome, simply by using the step-by-step approach described in this book, eg

- having systems to warn of the occurrence of problems
- defining and analysing problems adequately
- collecting all the relevant information
- questioning whether you have used inaccurate information or made assumptions about what is and isn't relevant
- asking for other people's points of view
- using models to represent the relationships between different aspects of the problem.

Emotional blocks

These can be difficult to overcome because they require a change in attitude, which may take some time to learn. The following methods help to achieve this change:

- accept that if you are looking for new, better ways of doing something, some mistakes are almost inevitable
- remember that many great thinkers have been ridiculed for what turned out to be great inventions eg the heavier-than-air flying machine
- if you still fear looking foolish, try to develop your ideas into a practical form before you show them to anyone, or develop a logical argument to prove that they will work

- following a strictly methodical approach will automatically curb impatience
- to avoid anxiety tackle problems in small, easily manageable steps; if necessary, put the problem aside and come back to it later
- if you don't want to take risks, identify the worst possible consequences, and how likely they are to occur, and then try to find ways of preventing them
- if a problem doesn't seem challenging, try to imagine the greatest benefits that could be achieved if it was solved.

Intellectual blocks

To overcome the intellectual blocks described in this chapter you need to

- learn to be methodical
- practise using different types of 'language' to tackle problems
- practise using the various analytical and creative techniques described in this book.

Expressive blocks

Overcoming these blocks involves learning to

- identify which 'language' is most likely to help you solve a particular problem
- use languages in different ways, eg diagrams to represent problems normally described verbally
- ensure that when you explain ideas you have all the relevant information, it is accurate, and that you convey it all clearly
- develop a style of working with others which is not too forceful (so that people are more willing to listen to you) and not too passive (so that you learn how to influence people); showing enthusiasm for your ideas can help by infecting others with enthusiasm.

Environmental blocks

Overcoming these blocks is covered in Chapter 4, but briefly these are some of the methods you can use:

- if there is a climate of criticism, develop the strengths of your ideas and ways to overcome their weaknesses before you propose them; being careful how you describe it to others will also help to avoid premature criticism
- conduct your problem solving in an environment which suits you, ie comfortable and free of distractions likely to hinder you; this may mean setting aside some time when you can move away from your normal working environment
- if you feel people may not provide the help you need, try to identify the benefits to them of solving the problem before you ask for their help
- if pressure of work hinders you, set aside some time when you are free from other work to tackle the problem
- if your work is monotonous, introduce some variety by looking for different ways of doing the job; alternatively, look for varied tasks that could be delegated to you.

Cultural blocks

The following methods can be used to help overcome the various cultural blocks:

- critically question existing ideas and methods, looking for areas for improvement
- identify constraints and question their validity
- if you dislike change, do some 'wishful thinking' to see what benefits change would bring; ask yourself what would be the consequences of taking a new approach
- if you think fantasy and humour have no place in problem solving, practice using your day-dreams to develop your ideas; next time

someone cracks a joke about a situation, think about what new perspectives it creates

- if you think intuition is unreliable, think back over recent problems you have solved; did that first 'hunch' turn out to be close to your final solution?
- if you are in a very competitive environment, be careful how you explain your ideas to people competing with you; emphasise the likely benefits to them
- if there is a strong climate of cooperation, ask members of your group for their ideas and comments; share the problem with them.

If you fail to solve a problem effectively, look back over your thoughts and actions to see if a block hindered you. If it did, next time you can prepare to avoid it. By being constantly aware of the blocks that can occur and using the techniques described above to overcome them when they hinder your problem solving, you will find that gradually fewer and fewer blocks occur.

KEY
POINTS

- There is a range of factors known as blocks which can prevent you finding the most effective solutions to our problems.
- You can recognise blocks by their specific effects on your thinking and problem solving.
- When you recognise that a block exists you can overcome it by using the appropriate technique.

PROJECT

Use this page to make a list of the blocks to which you think you are most susceptible. It will act as a reminder to be on your guard when tackling problems.

Chapter 4

A good climate for problem solving

The success of a company can depend to a large extent on the ability of its staff to solve problems effectively, both in their day-to-day work and through innovation. This applies not only to senior management, but at all levels in an organisation.

It's not enough simply to teach effective problem solving techniques. **The working environment** has a very powerful influence on the individual's ability to solve problems effectively and it **needs to be supportive and stimulating**.

To be truly effective in your work and to contribute to the success of your organisation, you need to be aware of the influence of the working environment on problem solving. This enables you to

- recognise and overcome negative influences on your own problem solving, and
- help to create an environment which will support others in their problem solving.

How the working environment influences people

The influence of our working environment is subtle and diverse. In addition to the physical environment, the *processes and procedures* we are required to follow in our work and the *attitudes and values* of those around us *can help or hinder our problem solving*. This happens in many ways, for example

- at work we tend to adopt the general attitude towards problem solving
- we will only tackle problems which come to us through accepted channels
- we will be more motivated to solve problems in innovative ways if there is greater 'reward' than for producing a regular solution
- we will not take risks with new ideas if failure brings severe criticism.

Consider the influence of these two managers on their staff.

Manager A believes in having complete control over the department's work and keeps a check on how work is progressing. Things have to be done a certain way and staff who suggest other methods, even if they are more effective, have their ideas dismissed without reason.

Manager B likes to be in control of the department's work but respects that people like to work in their own way. Encouragement and support are given to anyone who has an idea for improving the way things are done, even if at first they seem unlikely to succeed.

The attitude of **Manager A** is likely to discourage staff from suggesting ideas. They will become discontented and perhaps even leave the organisation for a more stimulating and supportive environment. Staff working for **Manager B** feel that their ideas are appreciated and that they are valued personally as team members. This inspires them to search for ways of improving efficiency without being asked.

This is only one factor. The working environment is composed of many elements and it's important to consider how each could influence problem solving.

What factors shape the working environment?

The elements which compose the working environment can be divided broadly into three interdependent groups:

- the company's policies and procedures
- the style of management
- the physical environment.

 ## ACTIVITY

Try to name three factors in each of the following areas which would help to create an environment which promotes good problem solving.

Company policies and procedures.

1.

2.

3.

Style of management.

1.

2.

3.

GUIDELINES

You may recognise some of your ideas amongst the following factors which can stimulate and support good problem solving.

Company policies and procedures

Possessing good problem solving skills does not make people automatically use them to the benefit of the organisation. They need encouragement, support and guidance in applying them to the organisation's problems. This can be achieved through:

Commitment to innovation

Resistance to change has fallen dramatically over the past decade but many organisations are still reluctant to promote change actively as part of their business strategy. This is particularly true where it takes the organisation into new markets or requires high investment in new manufacturing plant or additional management services.

A commitment to innovation is essential to success in a competitive business world. All staff should be made aware of this commitment, which should be part of the organisation's policy, underpinning its business strategy and reflected throughout its operation. It should produce in individuals an expectation of high achievement through problem solving. This commitment can be reflected and supported in the following ways.

Systems and procedures

As organisations grow they develop more complex management structures which create hierarchies of responsibility and authority. Although this is important to the efficient management of the operation it can create barriers to people using their problem solving skills. There are several steps that can be taken to avoid these barriers while maintaining efficient management:

- reduce the constraints imposed on individuals by making rules and normal procedures and practices more flexible
- avoid anything which may frustrate an individual's attempts to apply their enthusiasm for problem solving
- give individuals responsibility for their work and the way they complete it, so that there is less double checking and they have the freedom to develop more effective ways of working
- provide systems which allow people to see their ideas through from conception to execution
- ensure that procedures for interdepartmental communication allow individuals access (when warranted) to the information and resources of departments other than their own
- give authority to every member of staff to suggest solutions to other people's problems.

Reward

This is essential in promoting originality and innovation. Research has shown that many people who leave a company to develop their business ideas (**entrepreneurs**) do so because their attempts to do it within the company have been frustrated and not because their financial reward is insufficient. Their main incentive is achievement rather than money.

Although reward for good ideas can be given through promotion or as a bonus through suggestion schemes, it has proved more effective to create a new career structure for these individuals. This provides them with the resources and freedom to develop their ideas, together with prestige and salary increases – reward without moving up the managerial hierarchy and without its burden of added responsibility. The term **intrapreneur** has been coined to describe these people.

Good communications

This ensures that all staff are aware of the information above. In addition it ensures that

- all staff know the company's business objectives, such as expansion, new markets, and so on, so that they can apply their problem solving skills in contributing to its future success
- individual successes are well known, so that others are inspired and encouraged
- all levels of management know the importance of encouraging their staff to apply their skills to solving the organisation's problems and exploiting opportunities.

More and more organisations are establishing the **intrapreneur system**, which originated in America and has been particularly successful in companies like 3M, Hewlett-Packard and General Motors. One feature of the system is the 'sponsor'. This is a person who ensures that a particular project receives the resources required, calms internal political troubles and gives general advice to the intrapreneur on topics such as how to present an idea to management.

An example of the system is operated at the Colgate Palmolive Company in New York. Intrapreneurs head a brand management system which is independent from the main brand management. It was set up to develop new uses and markets for small and dying brands. One of these was HandiWipes, which the intrapreneurs decided to sell directly to hospitals, day care centres and schools.

Company **suggestion schemes** can also encourage good problem solving, provided they are managed properly. The most effective system is where all staff are informed of specific problems which the company faces in reaching its business objectives, and are notified of the results of evaluation of the ideas that have been submitted. Usually a financial reward is given for ideas which are used, perhaps

10% of the yearly saving to the company up to a certain maximum. Ideas submitted which are not applicable immediately to a particular problem can be kept in an **ideas bank** which can be consulted for possible solutions each time a problem arises.

Quality circles are another way of encouraging staff to contribute to the success of their organisation through problem solving. They have many other benefits, such as greater job satisfaction, and are described in Chapter 8.

Style of management

As the example earlier in this chapter shows, the way in which people are managed can have a profound effect on their problem solving. The major things a manager can do to stimulate and support good problem solving are:

Delegate responsibility

People who have responsibility for and control over their work feel a greater commitment to ensuring that they work efficiently. Staff should be given the freedom to make decisions and to tackle problems without constantly having to get agreement from their manager. Some managers feel that this lessens their control over staff and their work. In fact, because people are more committed to their work, there is less need for control.

Delegate problems

Involving members of staff in solving a problem has several benefits:

- it provides experience from which they can learn
- it helps to make them feel that they are contributing to the goals of the organisation
- the manager gains other points of view on problems

- people who are involved in finding a solution to a problem feel more committed to implementing it.

Ensure good communications

Make sure that everyone knows about and has easy access to information about the company's business objectives, its markets and its current problems.

Set high standards of achievement

This not only provides a stimulating challenge for staff to use problem solving to improve their efficiency, but it also creates an environment where individuals feel that only the best is acceptable, so they begin to set their own high standards. In setting standards it's vital that individuals know exactly what minimum standard they are expected to achieve in particular tasks.

Avoid undue criticism of people's ideas

We all know from experience that criticism of our ideas can be dispiriting, particularly if the ideas are new or unusual and the critical person is in a position of authority.

We often tend to look for flaws in other people's ideas rather than the good points. This may be because it proposes unsettling change, but more often it's for personal or political reasons, such as jealousy or anger about ideas from juniors or those we are competing with, perhaps from another department.

Undue criticism of ideas has two effects. People soon learn not to waste their time suggesting ideas when they know they will get a rebuff and, more insidiously, they become over-cautious in their thinking, concentrating on the flaws in an idea before it is even developed.

You should listen carefully to people's ideas and not reject them without careful consideration. Even if they appear impractical at first, perhaps they could be adapted and improved. When ideas do turn out to be completely impractical, explain to the person concerned why it would not work.

Remove constraints

If there are standard rules and procedures in the organisation which hinder problem solving don't enforce them unless absolutely necessary.

Encourage risk-taking in situations where the consequences of failure can be tolerated

To find original, innovative solutions to problems people need the freedom to experiment and this is inherently risky. Remember, ideas are not actions so even the most outlandish ideas can be tolerated without harm. Risk-taking can be actively encouraged, by suggesting to people that they look for unusual solutions to a situation, or passively, by ensuring that you do not harshly criticise ideas which are obviously impractical.

Encourage expression

This is achieved by using a variety of tactics, eg

- make a deliberate effort to ask people for their ideas on problems that arise
- listen attentively when people come to you with ideas
- avoid undue criticism of impractical ideas.

Give recognition for good ideas

We all need reward for our efforts and it's important that people know there will be greater reward for innovative solutions to problems than for regular solutions. As well as recognition and appreciation, another type of reward is for people to see their ideas implemented.

Provide 'time out' for problem solving

While some people find being under pressure of work or a deadline a stimulus to problem solving, others find it a hindrance and need to feel relaxed. People should be given the opportunity to spend time free from the pressures of other work to tackle important problems.

Physical environment

We all know from experience that our surroundings can have an important influence on the way we feel, think and work. This is particularly true of solving problems, in terms of both the process itself and the general attitude to productivity.

   ACTIVITY

Think about the type of physical environment you would find most suitable for solving problems and list its features below.

GUIDELINES

The type of physical environment we favour for problem solving is a very personal matter, according to what factors create in us the right state of mind for a particular task. For example, the bathroom is often reported as a site of inspiration, probably because it's a time when we are relaxed and distracted from concentration on a problem.

Most people require a different state of mind when they need to think creatively compared with doing analytical work. Analytical thinking requires concentration on the details of a problem, while creative thinking usually requires a more relaxed, free-ranging attitude.

Environmental stimuli can affect the ease with which we can use various mental skills. There is a biological mechanism through which physical stimulation automatically increases concentration up to a certain point, but beyond which it reduces our ability to concentrate. We each have a different optimum of environmental stimulation for both creative and analytical thinking.

We need to learn, through experience, what conditions suit us best and try to recreate those conditions each time we have a problem to tackle. This does not mean, for example, dashing to the bathroom every time we get stuck with a problem and need inspiration. We simply need to *recreate the state of mind which we find most effective for solving problems*.

In general terms, the following factors should be considered as important in the working environment:

Physical comfort
This is essential and should include a comfortable, even temperature; good lighting to avoid eyestrain; ergonomically designed furniture and office systems; low levels of noise; and minimum 'through traffic'.

Well planned space

Creating a 'light and airy' environment, rather than one which makes people feel enclosed and restricted, has a beneficial effect on people's state of mind. This includes avoiding overcrowding, providing natural light wherever possible and adequate storage and filing facilities to reduce clutter and give the appearance of order.

Good office resources

Lack of resources can cause uneccessary frustrations, so the easy availability of photocopiers, typing facilities, efficient means of communication and other necessary resources is important.

Does your organisation encourage and support problem solving?

This section will help you to assess the general attitude towards problem solving in your organisation.

    ACTIVITY

For each of the following statements, circle the number on the six-point scale which most accurately reflects the situation in your organisation. The more applicable the statement the higher the score.

	False				True	
All staff are made aware that it is the organisation's policy to promote and support originality and innovation.	1	2	3	4	5	6
People can follow their ideas through from conception to execution.	1	2	3	4	5	6
	1	2	3	4	5	6

The organisation successfuly operates schemes to promote problem solving activities eg a 'suggestion scheme, quality circles.

There is good communication between ranks.　　　1　2　3　4　5　6

People are given a large amount of responsibility for their work.　　　1　2　3　4　5　6

Reasonable risk-taking is encouraged.　　　1　2　3　4　5　6

People are more concerned with new ideas than with defending their turf.　　　1　2　3　4　5　6

Good ideas are rewarded, either by recognition, promotion or financially.　　　1　2　3　4　5　6

There are no barriers to communication between departmental functions.　　　1　2　3　4　5　6

There are no barriers to using resources from other departments.　　　1　2　3　4　5　6

Mistakes are tolerated in the cause of innovation.　　　1　2　3　4　5　6

The organisation makes a high investment in providing good facilities and pleasant surroundings.　　　1　2　3　4　5　6

Specific training for problem solving is available to staff.　　　1　2　3　4　5　6

Resources are set aside specifically for people to develop new ideas.　　　1　2　3　4　5　6

　　　1　2　3　4　5　6

Details of the organisation's current business objectives are made known to all staff.

Failure is regarded as a learning opportunity rather than an occasion for criticism.

1 2 3 4 5 6

Senior management seek out new ideas in every part of the organisation.

1 2 3 4 5 6

Red tape is kept to a minimum.

1 2 3 4 5 6

All staff are regularly informed of current problems facing the organisation.

1 2 3 4 5 6

In the cause of progress, senior management turns a blind eye to infringement of rules, procedures and practices.

1 2 3 4 5 6

The success of individuals' ideas are reported regularly to all staff.

1 2 3 4 5 6

Management receive training in how to encourage and support problem solving in the organisation.

1 2 3 4 5 6

GUIDELINES

This questionnaire is only a rough guide because it does not cover all of the factors which reflect an organisation's attitude to problem solving. However, the 'ideal' score – reflecting an organisation that actively encourages and supports problem solving – would be a '6' in answer to every question. **How does your organisation rate?**

If you feel more could be done in your organisation to promote and support problem solving, you may have the authority and resources to implement some of the methods described earlier in this chapter. However, even if you don't, there are many other ways in which you can help to make your working environment more supportive and stimulating.

How much encouragement and support are you giving?

Whatever your role in an organisation you can influence the working environment through your relationships with colleagues.

ACTIVITY

Read the following statements and tick those which apply to you. Be honest!

1. I like to get people involved in solving departmental problems.

2. I think it's dangerous to take risks in a business environment.

3. I regularly ask people for their ideas on important work issues.

4. When I'm working on a problem I don't like outside interference.

5. I give people as much responsibility as my authority allows.

6. I prefer people to use tried and tested methods.

7. When I've got a problem I like to share it with others and get their points of view.

8. I believe a manager's role is to direct and control the way work is done.

9. Even when someone suggests an idea which is obviously impractical I try to offer encouragement.

10. I discourage people from following hunches.

11. I welcome any suggestions for making work easier.

12. I think people should stick to their own work and not get involved in things which don't concern them.

13. I'm prepared to stretch the rules if there is a good reason.

14. I don't have patience with people who are always trying to dream up 'better' ways of doing things.

15. If someone had an idea which would benefit the organisation I would put them in touch with people who could help to develop it.

16. Other than getting their work completed on time and to a reasonable standard I don't push people too hard.

17. When things go wrong I help people analyse why rather than blaming anyone.

18. When things are working well I don't see any reason to change them.

19. I set increasingly high standards for people to achieve in their work.

20. When someone makes a mistake I would rather be blunt about it to discourage them from making the same mistake again.

GUIDELINES

Transfer your answers to the question numbers listed below. Give yourself one point for each question you have ticked and add up the total in each column.

1	2
3	4
5	6
7	8
9	10
11	12
13	14
15	16
17	18
19	20
———	———
———	———
encouraging and supportive	**discouraging and non-supportive**

Your score will give you some idea of the effect your actions and attitudes may be having on the problem solving efforts of your staff and colleagues. The project at the end of this chapter asks you to make a list of the things you can do to be more encouraging and supportive, based on the principles described in this chapter.

The problem solving skills of all staff is one of an organisation's key resources and needs to be managed efficiently. It has to be nurtured, developed and directed towards solving the problems facing the organisation.

KEY
POINTS

- Effective problem solving requires a stimulating and supportive environment.
- Aspects of the organisation's policies and procedures, the style of management and the physical environment can help or hinder problem solving.
- Whatever your role, you can help to create an environment which encourages and supports effective problem solving.

PROJECT

Make a list here of the things you will do to make your working environment more stimulating and supportive of good problem solving.

Does your list include *everything* that you could do?

Chapter 5

So what's the problem?

Before you start trying to solve a problem you need to be sure that a problem exists, discover precisely what it is, and decide whether it is important enough to warrant time and effort in solving it. This chapter will help you to

- ensure that you recognise problems efficiently
- define problems effectively
- decide if action is necessary and when.

Recognising problems

Some problems arise suddenly, without warning, and are painfully obvious by their effects. Others develop more slowly, perhaps over many days, weeks or months, and have a more subtle influence. On some occasions, what you think is a problem may turn out not to be a problem at all. It's important to be able to recognise problems efficiently.

Bill Pearce was asked to produce an urgent report on his department's use of company resources. Normally he asked Brian or Julia to research and write reports, but Brian had left the previous week and Julia was on maternity leave. Asking round his staff for someone to delegate the task to, Bill discovered that none of them had ever written a report before. The result was that he had to ask for an extension of the deadline until he had time to write it himself.

Bill's situation highlights *the way in which some problems develop*. Producing reports was a regular feature of the department's work. The request for a report to be written would arrive and that objective would normally be achieved by Julia or Brian. So the **objective** went through phases – latent (before a report was requested), current (when it had to be written), then latent again (once the report had been written and before another was requested).

Similarly, the **obstacle** (the lack of someone with experience in writing reports) went through phases. It was developing, though still latent, when Julia went on leave. It became effective when Brian left and would have become latent again when Julia returned from maternity leave.

All objectives and obstacles go through phases to some extent, and a problem arises when a current objective coincides with an effective obstacle. The growth and decay of objectives and obstacles varies tremendously. For example, industrial unrest which leads to strike action may have been growing for many months or years. Similarly, annual sales targets are achieved gradually over twelve months and may undergo seasonal and monthly variations.

If you can monitor the growth and decay of objectives and potential obstacles you will be in a position to take action to prevent a problem occurring, or at least be prepared to tackle it immediately when it arises.

 ACTIVITY

Think about your areas of responsibility at work and answer the following questions.

How do you become aware of problems?

What enables you to detect problems?

Briefly describe two methods you could use which would help you to recognise problems earlier and more effectively.

GUIDELINES

You should never be in the position of facing a problem which could have been foreseen or, worse still, not recognising that a problem exists. Recognising problems efficiently involves being aware of the areas in which they may arise and establishing specific methods of detection. The following methods will help you to detect problems early:

Monitor performance
You can detect any shortfall in agreed standards or targets by monitoring performance. This means first ensuring that all staff know precisely what standards of work and behaviour they are required to maintain, and setting up systems to measure the standards achieved.

Observe staff
By doing this you can detect changes in behaviour which may reflect an underlying problem.

Listen to staff
Try to be aware of any concerns staff may have in their work or their relationships with others, both inside and outside work.

Review and compare
If you regularly review and compare past performance and behaviour with the current situation you can detect gradual deterioration.

There are many methods of measuring performance, from simple subjective judgements made about an individual's behaviour, to sophisticated point of sale computer monitoring systems used by multiple retailers. Whatever methods you use, it's important that you *don't jump to conclusions* about the data they provide. Until you investigate the situation you can't be sure that a problem exists or you may assume the cause incorrectly.

To help you recognise opportunities , you can supplement the list above by looking at your major areas of responsibility and asking yourself questions such as:

- Could we exceed the current targets and objectives?
- Could I utilise the resources within my control more efficiently?
- Are there new objectives that could be set?

You can ask the same questions of colleagues, other departments and the organisation as a whole, looking for opportunities in terms of both performance (such as output, efficiency and profitability) and the personal needs of staff (such as safety, comfort and job satisfaction).

The primary area for *identifying new objectives for the organisation* is in market terms – what does the market need that we could supply? In a sense you are looking at other people's problems that you could solve, either by supplying a new product or service or improving an existing one.

There is a wealth of data available on business markets but this can be misleading, particularly where new products are concerned. Art Fry, inventor of the now familiar 'Post-it' notes, was told by the marketing department at 3M that there was no market for them. Undeterred, he went directly to potential customers and asked for their views. This market research supported his belief in his invention and encouraged 3M to produce and market the product.

The most direct way to identify market needs is to approach customers and potential customers and ask what problems they have with existing products or services, and what needs they have that you could fill with a new product or service.

When you have recognised that a problem exists, you should *decide who has responsibility for the situation*, ie who 'owns' it. If a problem is not your direct responsibility you will need to inform the owner. You may be asked to deal with it anyway, but the owner may have the information or resources needed to find an effective solution, or you may need approval later to implement your solution. You could also be asked to solve a problem for someone else, or to contribute to its solution. However you become involved in solving a problem, you must ensure that it is defined effectively.

Defining problems

When you first become aware of a problem it is often as a hazy notion that things are not as they should be, or that they could be improved. To deal with the situation effectively you need to describe or define it as something which you can act upon. These definitions vary in complexity but their primary function is to point you in the right direction for further work on the problem. They help you to

- identify a tangible target to be achieved
- reduce complex problems to a series of smaller problems
- focus on the important aspects of a problem
- assess its importance and allocate appropriate resources to solve it
- explain the problem to others who may be involved or can help in its solution
- locate clues to possible strategies and solutions
- define the type of information you require
- define criteria for measuring the potential effectiveness of various solutions.

To define a problem effectively you need to gather information about the situation. The method which detected the problem will provide enough information to enable you to make a preliminary definition. For example, you may have observed that 'Jane and Iain are having difficulty working together'. This will tell you what type of further information you need and where to look for it. Usually you need to redefine the problem, perhaps several times, as your understanding of the problem grows.

Closed and open-ended problems are usually defined in different ways. With closed problems, where finding a solution first involves finding the cause, the emphasis is on identifying and specifying the possible causes. Open-ended problems, where there are many possible solutions, require a definition which broadens the search for solutions. Defining closed problems is an analytical, convergent process. Defining open-ended problems is a more creative, divergent process.

Defining closed problems

Defining closed problems involves identifying and recording all aspects of the deviation from the norm, from which you can begin to deduce the possible causes. A preliminary definition of a closed problem might be, for example, 'quality control has detected a 15% increase in rejects of component A during the past week'. This type of definition is of little help in locating the cause of such a problem, but it's a starting point for making a detailed description of the situation.

A technique widely used for defining closed problems is the Kepner–Tregoe approach, which helps to systematically analyse and define all aspects of the problem situation. Developed by Drs Kepner and Tregoe, it was used by Kepner to help find the cause of the explosion on board the Apollo space capsule in 1968, which killed three American astronauts. The cause of the accident was eventually isolated in the explosive mixture of gases used. Although this may seem an obvious place to look, bearing in mind that the lives of other astronauts could have been at risk subsequently, it was essential that every possibility of other causes or contributing factors was ruled out.

The Kepner–Tregoe approach consists of answering a series of questions about the situation, such as: What is the problem?; What isn't the problem?; Where is the problem?;

Where isn't the problem? The answers help to build a detailed definition of the problem.

 # ACTIVITY

This is based on the Kepner–Tregoe approach. The sales director of a chain of department stores has detected a dramatic fall in sales in one department of a particular store. This information came from the computerised point of sale system which provides him with up-to-the-minute details of sales in the departments of each store. A preliminary definition of the problem is given below. Write down how you think the sales director might answer the remaining questions.

What is the problem?

There has been a 75.8% fall in sales over the past three days in the cosmetics and toiletries department at the Birmingham store

---

What isn't the problem?

What is distinctive about it?

Where is the problem?

_____

Where isn't the problem?

_____

Who/what does the problem involve?

_____

Who/what doesn't the problem involve?

_____

When did or when does the problem occur?

_____

When didn't or when doesn't it occur?

Now look back through your answers and think about what they tell you about the problem.

GUIDELINES

Without being able to investigate the situation you can only guess at answers to some of the questions, but this demonstrates how the method is used to clarify problems and to suggest possible causes. For example, in answer to the question 'Who/what does the problem involve?' you could have written: cosmetics and toiletries at the Birmingham store, cash terminals in the cosmetics and toiletries department and the staff who operate them. This immediately suggests possible causes, such as problems with the stock, a fault in the equipment, or its inaccurate use by staff. In this case the cause of the problem was eventually identified as the faulty transmission of data from the cash terminal to the central computer.

The questions can be modified to adapt to different situations and a detailed analysis using this method would include **additional questions** such as

- What is the same when the problem occurs?
- What is different when the problem occurs?
- What is the extent of the problem?
- Is the problem getting bigger?
- Is the problem getting smaller?
- What is distinctive about its change in size?

In combination, the answers to these questions build up a detailed picture of the problem which often suggests possible causes. However, when you use the Kepner–Tregoe method it's important not to jump to conclusions about the likely causes. You must complete the analysis because you locate the true cause of the problem later by testing each possibility to see if it fits all the circumstances. However, you should note any possible causes which occur to you at this stage.

When applying this method to your own problems you

will need to investigate the situation carefully in order to answer the questions accurately, and all the information which supports your answers should be documented so that it can be verified later. Questions may be asked repeatedly as your understanding of the problem grows, so that you can define it more precisely.

Although the Kepner–Tregoe method is time consuming and not easy to use at first, it is worth persevering with because it ensures that you define closed problems carefully and thoroughly.

Defining open-ended problems

An open-ended problem is defined in terms of goals or objectives as *a statement of what you want to achieve by solving the problem*. The definition needs to be precise, to give clear direction to your search for solutions, but at the same time to identify all the possible goals which would contribute to your overall objective. Therefore open-ended problems are best defined in two stages – first to explore all the possible goals and then to define precisely those which you want to achieve.

Defining the problem in terms of a 'How to ... ?' statement, eg 'How to finance expansion?', focuses attention on the problem area and provides a basis for suggesting alternative goals and routes to a solution.

 ACTIVITY

This is based on a 'test' devised Dr Tudor Rickards, Director of the Creativity Programme at Manchester Business School.

1. Write down a preliminary definition of an open-ended problem that you have faced or are facing currently. Phrase it in terms of 'How to ... ?'.

How to ...

2. Take as much time as you want and complete the following statements.

There is usually more than one way of looking at a problem. You can define this one as ...

But the main point of the problem is ...

What I would really like to do is ...

If I could break all the rules and laws of reality I would try to solve it by ...

The problem put in any other way could be likened to ...

Another, even stranger way of looking at it might be ...

Now look at your original definition. Do any of your redefinitions help you to see the problem in a different and perhaps more effective way?

GUIDELINES

If you 'tested' many different open-ended problems you would find that usually they do not have a single 'correct' definition. For example, 'How to increase sales?' could be restated as

How to ... make our product more saleable?
          increase sales outlets?
          improve our market share?
          make our marketing more effective?
          make our sales team more effective?

Trying to find a single all-encompassing definition severely limits the scope of possible solutions. Sometimes what appears to be a single problem is in fact a collection of several smaller, related problems.

Inaccurate or misleading definitions can result in ineffective solutions . A company which defines its major problem as 'How to overcome the shortage of specialist skills amongst staff?' may decide to solve it by recruiting people with those skills. In some situations this may be the best solution. However, if the problem is caused by the resignation of trained personnel – through low pay, poor working conditions, lack of promotion prospects, or whatever – the original definition would be inadequate and misleading.

An effective definition accurately represents the key features of the problem in a way which gives direction to your work in solving it, and problem situations have to be investigated thoroughly before they can be defined effectively. Some of the techniques covered in Chapter 7 can be used to help generate alternative 'How to ...' statements. In brainstorming and Synectics (Chapter 8) these preliminary definitions are used to stimulate the generation of ideas for a solution, but normally they need to be restated more precisely.

The more precise the definition, the greater your chances of finding an effective solution. Compare these two statements:

How to improve my efficiency at work?

Within six months I want to complete reports within 3 days instead of the 5 days it takes me currently, reduce the average time I spend in meetings each week from 7 hours to 4 hours ...

The first statement gives little information about the problem and doesn't tell you where to look for solutions. The second statement tells you exactly what you are achieving now and what you want to achieve, giving a clear indication of the gap you need to bridge in solving the problem.

The same is true of statements about obstacles. The more clearly they are defined the easier it is to find ways to deal with them. Answering the following questions will help you to define obstacles:

- What is the obstacle?
- How did it arise?
- What are its dimensions?
- What are its effects?
- It is growing or diminishing?
- Is it temporary or permanent?

To write your detailed definition, first select the 'How to ...?' statements which most accurately represent your problem. Then, for each one, make separate *lists of the characteristics of the current situation and the desired situation* (where your objective will have been achieved). Whenever possible these characteristics should be stated in measurable terms, so that you know what will constitute a successful solution, how soon it will be achieved, and how you will measure your success. Next, *add details of any obstacles* and how they prevent you reaching your objective.

It's also important to consider what effect your efforts to reach your objectives, and actually reaching them, would have on others. This involves doing a **needs analysis** , which documents how changing the current situation into the desired one affects others, including the organisation. One of the objectives of a manager wanting to manage his time more effectively, for example, may be to spend less time 'walking the job'. This means less direct contact with his staff and less opportunity for them to discuss their problems.

Depending on the situation, you can either modify your objectives or set secondary objectives to accommodate the needs of others. This manager, for example, might institute a regular 'surgery' for discussions with staff. Differences in needs can also be reconciled through negotiation, use of authority, and so on.

Use this checklist to review how thoroughly you have defined a problem .

- Can this objective be divided into several sub-goals?
- Is this objective the ultimate goal in solving the problem?
- Is achieving this objective simply a route to achieving another objective?
- Are there other related objectives?
- Can this obstacle be sub-divided?
- Does this obstacle really prevent me reaching this objective?
- Are there other related obstacles?
- Does this obstacle prevent me reaching other objectives?
- Does this definition take account of the needs of others who are involved or who may be affected?

Open-ended problems are related to a need or desire to improve upon the current situation and *there is an inevitable risk that you may fail to benefit, or even change the situation for the worse.* As a safeguard against this happening you should make a detailed comparison of the benefits of the current situation with those you will achieve by reaching your objectives. This will enable you to look for solutions which retain the good features of the current situation. You should be prepared to forfeit these only when they are clearly outweighed by the benefits of achieving your objectives. This type of analysis will also help you to measure the potential gain and estimate the practical limit of your resources in finding a solution.

Many of the techniques described for defining open-ended problems can be applied to defining closed problems once their cause (the obstacle) has been identified.

Defining problems effectively often requires painstaking work. You can't afford to make assumptions or dive straight into looking for a solution. Sometimes the process of defining a problem reveals that it doesn't require any action, perhaps because it will disappear and not recur, or because the actual loss or potential gain is relatively insignificant. On other occasions you may need to decide when it would be best to act.

Is action necessary, and when?

The effects of some problems are not significant enough to merit time and effort in solving them. Even when they do, because many objectives and obstacles go through phases of growth and decay, *tackling a problem immediately may not be the best course of action.* For example, if rain is preventing you painting your house you wait until it stops raining rather than trying to erect a huge canopy over the house. When you have a problem there are a number of options open to you, depending on the nature of the situation:

Do nothing: when the problem will solve itself; when its effects are insignificant; when the cost of solving it is greater than the potential gain.

Monitor the situation: when it is not urgent; when the problem is diminishing; when you are unsure of the cause; when you need time to plan what to do; when the obstacle is getting smaller; when the objective is developing or declining and finding a solution is likely to be difficult.

Deal with the effects: when the cause will subside; when the cost of removing the cause is too great; when an obstacle is too intractable.

Try to solve it immediately: when the problem is growing; when it is having serious effects; when the obstacle is getting larger; when the objective is developing or declining and finding a solution is likely to be relatively easy; when a deadline has been imposed.

You can use the grid shown in Fig. 5.1 to help you to decide whether to act now or to wait. Answers to the questions are scored as high (3), medium (2) or low (1).

What is the extent of the benefits offered by solution?			What is the extent of the losses if I don't act?	
What are the chances of the benefits diminishing?			What are the chances of the benefits growing?	
At what rate will they diminish?			At what rate will they grow?	
What are the chances of the losses growing?			What are the chances of the losses diminishing?	
At what rate will they grow?			At what rate will they diminish?	
	ACT			WAIT

Figure 5.1

The highest scoring column indicates whether you should act now or wait. Although this grid can be used accurately in many situations, there may be overriding factors which you need to consider, such as deadlines imposed by internal or external authorities.

This grid can also be used when you face *several problems which all appear to need your immediate attention*. Trying to tackle them all at the same time runs a high risk of spreading your time too thinly and not finding an effective solution to any of them. If some of the problems can't be delegated to others then you need to *tackle them in order of priority*.

Establishing priorities involves estimating the relative importance of the effects of action versus inaction for each problem. Using the grid to analyse each problem, the scores in the left-hand column will tell you the relative urgency of acting on each one. Again there may be overriding factors, such as one problem having to be solved first to facilitate the solution of another.

When you have decided to act upon a problem, the search for solutions involves finding ways to close the gap between your current situation and one where you will have achieved your objective. At any stage it may be necessary to redefine the problem, or you may decide that, due to new information you have acquired, or due to a change in circumstances, the problem does not require further action. The methods used to find a solution are described in Chapter 6.

KEY
POINTS

- To recognise problems efficiently you need to establish and maintain specific methods of detection.
- To deal with problems effectively you need first to define it as something you can act upon.
- It's not always appropriate to try to solve a problem immediately.
- If you face several problems at once you may need to decide which one to tackle first.

PROJECT

Think of an open-ended problem (including opportunities) that you are currently facing and write a definition of it below using the methods described in this chapter. You will need this definition for the project in Chapter 6.

Chapter 6

Finding possible solutions

Finding a solution to a problem involves constructing a course of action that will transform your current situation into one where your objective has been achieved. Some problems require no further analysis once they have been defined effectively. If the definition confirms that it's a common or routine problem, such as the failure of a component in a manufacturing plant or a situation requiring disciplinary action, it can be solved by implementing the appropriate standard solution.

Less common and more complex problems require further analysis. Even though the definition may have given you clues to some possible solutions, you should explore all the possibilities. There is considerable overlap between the stages involved but the process of finding solutions can be represented as a cycle (see Figure 6.1).

If you have not already done so, at this stage you must *decide who else should be involved in solving the problem and in what way*. This may be people involved with or affected by the problem, with experience of, or an interest in, this type of situation, with relevant knowledge, or with good problem solving skills. In Chapter 8 there is a list of questions which will help you to decide whether a particular problem would be tackled best using group problem solving.

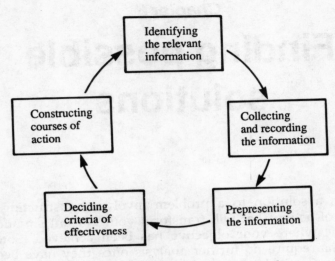

Figure 6.1 Problem solving cycle

Identifying the relevant information

The purpose of this stage is to give structure to your search for information and ideas relevant to the problem. You need to decide what information you require, where you can find it, and how you can gather it most effectively. With open-ended problems this information will help you to deal with obstacles and find ways to achieve your objectives. For closed problems you need information which will help you to clarify the problem, identify the cause, and suggest possible solutions.

ACTIVITY

Imagine you have defined a problem. Briefly describe how you will decide what further information you require.

GUIDELINES

If you have defined the problem adequately you will already have some of the information required, based on who and what is involved. Your objectives, any obstacles, and your description of the current and desired situations will help you to identify the type of information you require and possible sources. In the case of closed problems you would look first at your answers to the questions in the Kepner–Tregoe analysis and any possible causes which they suggest.

Two other useful sources of information are past experience of similar problems and people involved with or affected by the problem who may have relevant information. It's vital to distinguish between facts, ideas, needs, opinions and prejudices, although you must not ignore any information relevant to the problem. If several people express the same need, for example, collectively it may represent an important factor in finding an effective solution.

Your *information must be relevant to the problem, accurate and preferably quantified*. Ultimately, you need to answer the following questions:

- What type of information is required, eg financial, strategic, technical, policy, behavioural?
- What specific information is required, eg dates, times, amounts, names, actions?
- Why is this information required, eg to clarify the situation, to identify resources for solving the problem?
- What are the sources of this information, eg yourself, colleagues, eye-witnesses, records, specialists, other departments, books, researchers?
- What form will it take, eg numerical, statistical, verbal?

- How accurate or reliable are the sources, eg are they biased, is the information in the form of opinions?
- How can this information be obtained, eg memos, reports, meetings, informal discussions, observation, listening, testing?

As you answer these questions you should draw up a list of the specific information you require, where you can find it, and how you can gather it most effectively.

It's often difficult to recall from memory all the important factors relating to a particular problem. You can use many of the creative techniques described in Chapter 7 to help you identify relevant information and the possible causes of closed problems.

Collecting and recording the information

Information should be gathered and recorded systematically, starting with that which is going to take the longest time to collect, eg advice from an outside expert. The information should be recorded as it is gathered and not left to the memory. Any information you have not gathered yourself should be verified eg finding out the original source of the information and how it was collected. It's particularly important to verify quantified data.

A regional director had prepared a budget using a cost analysis of the various functions under her control, partly based on data supplied by five area managers. Two days after submitting the budget to her managing director she received a memo from him saying that the projections were totally unacceptable and not in line with other regions.

Investigating the reasons for the discrepancy, the regional director found that one area manager had presented his figures to her in such a way as to inflate his actual data processing costs in order to provide extra funds the following year.

Apart from any errors you may make in the collection and analysis of information, numerical and statistical data can be manipulated by others to serve their own interests. You must ensure that the way information is presented to you reflects the true situation and that any conclusions offered about its relevance are accurate and logical.

Representing the information

Information relevant to the problem now needs to be organised into a meaningful pattern. With complex problems it's impossible to hold all the information in your mind and to think about it clearly. Even with simple problems it's invaluable to have a tangible representation or **model of the problem** which gives structure to the information. Various types of model are described in Chapter 7. These help to

- reveal relationships between different aspects of the problem
- highlight gaps in your information and understanding
- stimulate your search for solutions
- communicate understanding to other people
- predict the likely consequences of actions you think may solve the problem.

At this stage you should have a detailed understanding of the problem. If you are dealing with a **closed problem** you should have a list of possible causes, together with all the information supporting or refuting each cause. To ensure that this list is comprehensive you can use the five sources of ideas listed on page 116.

To identify the real cause of the problem you test each possible cause against the effects noted in your analysis. By a process of elimination the real cause is identified as the one which has precisely the same effects as those which have occurred. If none of them fits precisely it means that either your definition is inadequate or you need to look for other causes.

Defining criteria of effectiveness

Before looking for solutions to a problem it is important to decide what will constitute an effective solution. This involves compiling a detailed list of the characteristics of what you want to achieve and of the factors which must be taken into account in achieving that objective, ie an 'ideal' solution. These criteria of effectiveness *give direction to your search for solutions*, telling you whether you are on the right track, and will help you later to measure the relative effectiveness of your solutions.

 ACTIVITY

Think about what 'solving' a problem actually means and then make a list of all the factors you may need to consider in deciding what would be an 'effective' solution.

GUIDELINES

Some of the information you need, though generally not all of it, may be stated in the problem definition. You need to consider a complex mixture of factors. An 'effective' solution must

- provide an acceptable level of benefits in terms of the objective
- deal effectively with obstacles/causes
- meet constraints on time, space, manpower and materials
- be cost effective and affordable
- be acceptable to
  - those affected by the problem and the solution (eg staff, customers, clients, suppliers)
  - those who have to agree to the solution
  - those who will provide the necessary resources
  - those who have to implement the solution
- involve an acceptable level of risk.

Some of these factors, such as the risks involved, can only be defined accurately when you have found a specific course of action, although your knowledge of the background to the problem situation should give you some guidance. Other factors, such as cost constraints, can be defined broadly before you look for solutions, even though later you may find a solution offering benefits which warrant changing the constraints.

At this stage of problem solving these criteria only serve as a *guide* in finding solutions which fit the circumstances and are likely to succeed. *You must not allow them to inhibit your search for solutions.*

Constructing courses of action to solve the problem

Finding possible solutions now involves constructing courses of action which meet your criteria of effectiveness as closely as possible. Inevitably, different approaches to solving a problem will provide different mixes of advantages and disadvantages.

You can start your search for solutions by constructing a chart based on your analysis of the problem (Figure 6.2). This shows all the changes required to achieve the various components of your objective. One aspect of your objective, for example, may be to raise employee awareness of your company's markets.

Current situation	Desired situation	Change required	Means of change
Employee awareness of company markets only 28%	Employee awareness of company markets at least 85%	Raise employee awareness of company markets to at least 85%	Seminars Video Involve employees in solving sales and marketing departments' problems

Figure 6.2

The details of each means of change or part-solution need to be elaborated to show how they will achieve the change required and to show their associated disadvantages. You then add details of how you could minimise these disadvantages. One of the obstacles in using seminars, for example, may be the widespread geographical locations of employees. One method of overcoming this may be to hold several regional seminars, close to local offices.

Although your ideas must eventually meet your criteria of effectiveness, these can inhibit idea generation. The best approach is to create as many ideas as possible for achieving each of the changes required and only test them against these criteria once you have explored all the possibilities. Cost, for example, may be one of the constraints on using video to raise employee awareness of company markets. Once you have identified video as a possible solution you can consider how you could meet the cost constraint, eg by producing the video in-house.

There are basically five sources of ideas for solving a problem and you should use as many of them as possible:

- past experience of similar situations
- logical deduction from the facts
- other people
- published sources
- creative idea generation techniques (see Chapter 7).

As you search for solutions, answering the following questions will help you to explore all the possibilities:

- Do I really need to achieve this objective?
- Could I substitute a different objective?
- Could I achieve this objective in a different way?
- Would there be any advantage in delaying trying to achieve this objective?
- Would someone else be more effective in achieving this objective?
- Is this really an obstacle?
- Would someone else be more effective in dealing with this obstacle?
- Can I deal with the causes of this obstacle?
- Can I side-step this obstacle?

- Can I use this obstacle to my advantage?

Each action that you propose will be intended to achieve a particular effect. In doing so it may also have *side-effects which can be desirable or undesirable*. If possible you should build into your solution ways to minimise undesirable side-effects and to take advantage of the desirable ones. Introducing new technology to improve efficiency, for example, may necessitate training. In turn, this could be an opportunity to reorganise the associated out-dated procedures. Similarly, an in-store promotion can be used to influence public perception of the company at the same time as promoting products.

As you build up different plans of action you can use an appropriate model to represent how each action contributes to achieving your overall objective. Models also help you to predict the effects of various actions and to see how they interact. It's important that the actions form a coherent strategy for tackling the problem. When several actions have to run consecutively, for example, you need to ensure that together they will meet any time constraints which exist.

Once you have constructed a range of possible solutions you need to *consider what could influence their effectiveness* eg.

- What could go wrong? (eg does the person you are relying upon to negotiate the contract have enough experience?)
- Are there related factors over which I have no control? (eg government legislation, organisational policy changes)
- Could this objective change? (eg are new, higher targets likely to be set before this solution is implemented?)
- Could this obstacle become more intractable? (eg with the imminent reorganisation of the department could this person become even more uncooperative?)

- Could relevant new obstacles arise? (eg a change in market needs, a competitor using the same solution)
- Might this action create a new opportunity which could be exploited at the same time? (eg could we market some of the information on this new database and offset some of our costs?)

Answers to these questions will help you to modify your solutions to minimise the chances of them failing and to optimise their benefits. When you have a number of solutions which you feel could achieve your objective effectively you have to evaluate them. This process is explained in Chapter 9.

KEY POINTS

- All information relevant to the problem must be identified, collected and recorded in a meaningful way.
- Identifying what constitutes an effective solution helps to guide your search for solutions.
- Finding solutions involves constructing courses of action which will transform the current situation into one where your objective is achieved.

PROJECT

Use the techniques described in this chapter to find possible solutions to the open-ended problem you defined in the project in Chapter 5. Remember to cover the following stages:

- Identify the relevant information.
- Collect and record the information.
- Represent the information in a meaningful way.
- Define your criteria of effectiveness.
- Construct courses of action.

Chapter 7

Representing problems and generating ideas

When we face an important problem our eagerness to solve it often leads us to accept the first solution that comes to mind, so that we can implement it without delay. Very often this will not be the most effective solution available. The best approach, particularly with open-ended problems, is to create a range of possible solutions from which we can subsequently select the best.

 ACTIVITY

Try to recall from your experience examples of the following two situations. Describe briefly what major difficulties you encountered. If you don't have experience of them, try to imagine the difficulties.

1. Tackling a very complex problem with many interrelated parts.

2. Finding a new, more effective solution to a very common problem.

GUIDELINES

These examples highlight two very common difficulties in finding the best solution to a problem:

1. *Not seeing all the relationships between different parts of the problem.* The human mind can focus on only a small amount of information at one time, so that we often find it difficult to hold a complete and detailed mental picture of a problem in our minds. Without this, we may overlook important relationships.

It's vital to know how all the parts of a problem are interrelated, otherwise we can waste time and perhaps not find the most effective solution. For example, our solution may aggravate the problem because we overlooked a particular relationship, or there may be a better solution involving two aspects we didn't relate.

2. *Not seeing beyond the most obvious solution.* The way we associate ideas and concepts in our minds, forming patterns which are reinforced by experience, often makes it hard to see common situations in a new light. Relationships between information which are new or seem 'unlikely', and ideas which appear irrelevant, may be either consciously excluded or not triggered from memory because of their weak associations with the situation.

To find creative solutions to our problems we need to escape habitual ways of looking at situations. The techniques described in this chapter will help you to

- **discover how elements of a problem are related**, by representing them in a tangible model
- **generate new ideas** by combining information in different ways.

Using models to represent problems

Models give shape and structure to information, making it easier to remember, think about and build on our ideas. They can highlight gaps in our information, help to predict the consequences of our actions and stimulate ideas. Models are also invaluable for communicating problems and ideas for their solution to other people.

In most situations you will find it helpful to use a model to represent the parts of a problem in an appropriate pattern. There are many different types, composed variously of words, graphics, mathematical formulae, symbols, and so on, as well as physical models.

There are various *standard models* which can be used to represent problems which have common elements linked by the same relationships. These can be applied to any problem which fits the model. Chemical equations and algebraic formulae are examples. So are *business games*, which represent details of a variety of business situations and predict the consequences of our actions according to how aspects of those situations interact in the real world.

Another example is *communication*, where the common elements are the originator, the sender, the message, the medium, and the receiver. Effective communication relies on an efficient flow of information from one end to the other. This model can be used to analyse a situation and identify exactly what is happening at each stage which may be preventing effective communication.

In addition to standard models, there is a wide range of options for representing problems.

Words as models

Words are the simplest and one of the most popular and flexible ways of representing a problem, either alone or in combination with pictorial or graphical elements.

The easiest way to create a word model is to list the main features of a problem, perhaps including associated ideas that come to mind. This can be updated and expanded as you think of additional relevant information. Word models can be manipulated easily, reordering the words in sequence or classifying them into groups, to highlight the relationships and differences between the information.

Abbreviated notes can be used effectively in the same way although prose, which is often used to describe a problem, is less effective. The more structure that exists in each descriptive unit, the less easy it is to add to and manipulate the information to reveal new relationships.

Words are easy to record and act as potent stimuli to the imagination. They are the most common way of communicating problems to other people. However, *there are some drawbacks*. The choice of a particular word or phrase to describe an idea can obscure its relationship with other relevant information. For example, if you use the word *box* to describe a 'container' you want to redesign it could narrow your thinking about different shapes and materials.

Also it is often difficult to give structure to the information contained in word models. Therefore it's a good idea not to use them alone, but perhaps as a preliminary to creating other types of model.

Drawings and diagrams

Drawing is an ideal way of beginning to create some kind of structure with your ideas. Unlike words alone, lines can represent relationships more easily and give concrete form to a problem.

In making a drawing to represent a problem you are not trying to create a work of art. It should be spontaneous, like doodling, allowing your thoughts to evolve in a visual way. Drawings can suggest new relationships between ideas, new ways of structuring a problem and new routes to a solution.

A more structured form of drawing is to create a diagram, such as those described in the remainder of this section. A very useful type is the mind map or Buzan diagram, described by Tony Buzan in his book *Use Your Head* (BBC Books, London 1986).

Mind maps

This is a visual method of structuring ideas which can take on almost any form. The main idea or concept is written at the centre of a page and then any related ideas that spring to mind are added as branches off this central point. As each one triggers more ideas they are added as connecting lines, branching outwards in all directions.

Ideas are written in block capitals along a line as it is added, so that each one acts as a clear trigger to the recall of associated ideas. The method capitalises on the brain's power of association, subsequent branches becoming more and more remote from the central idea.

The process should be spontaneous. You must not consciously think about where to place branches, whether to exclude an idea, or try to think of ways of extending a particular branch if nothing springs to mind. The aim is to record everything you can recall which may have the remotest relationship with the central idea (see Figure 7.1).

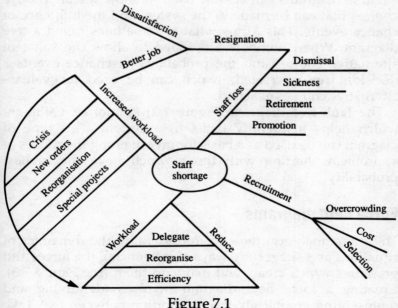

Figure 7.1

It is unlikely that a first attempt at drawing a mind map would look as tidy as the example in Figure 7.1, but very often a definite structure will emerge. If not, the ideas can be reordered quite easily. Mind maps are very effective both for representing the ramifications of a problem and for generating ideas for solutions.

Chain diagrams

These are created in a more logical way than mind maps and show clearly how the main elements of a problem are related. For example, it could show the stages in the manufacture of a product or the supply of a service, with the labour, time or cost involvement at each stage.

Chain diagrams can be very complicated, with feedback loops and so on, showing the different kinds of relationships between information. The direction of 'flow' of the process can be represented by arrows and numbers can be added to quantify what is happening at each stage.

These diagrams can also be used to show the alternative choices that can be made in the system and the influence of chance events. This forms what is sometimes called a **tree diagram**. When numbers are added to show the value of alternative choices and the probability of chance events a **decision tree** is created, which can be used to evaluate alternative courses of action.

The **fault-tree diagram** (Figure 7.2) is another variation, which helps to identify faults in a system. This type of diagram can be used as a basis for investigating the causes of a problem, starting with those which have the highest probability.

Force field diagrams

These are analytical tools for representing the dynamics of situations and suggesting ways of influencing the forces and pressures which create and maintain them (see Figure 7.3). Creating a force field diagram involves identifying and representing graphically the equilibrium between two Take

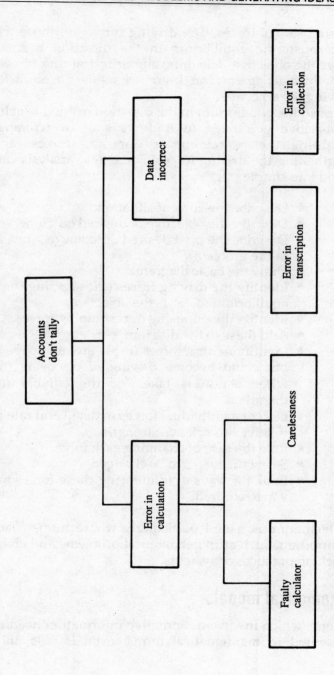

Figure 7.2 A fault-tree diagram

opposing sets of forces. The **driving forces** are those which would push the equilibrium in the direction needed to achieve the objective. The opposing or **restraining forces** are those which act against the desired change – the obstacles to achieving the objective.

To push the equilibrium in the direction needed to achieve the objective you need to find ways of overcoming or neutralising the restraining or opposing forces, and/or strengthening the driving forces. Force field analysis can be divided into simple stages:

- Describe the current situation.
- Describe the objective or desired outcome.
- Describe the least desired outcome (a worsening of the problem).
- Draw the basic diagram.
- Identify the driving forces (those acting to push equilibrium towards the objective).
- Identify the opposing or restraining forces.
- Add these to the diagram.
- Identify neutral forces (these are not active now but could become driving or opposing forces when action is taken or the equilibrium is disturbed).
- Describe individual forces in detail and rate their relative importance/strength.
- Rate the ease of changing each force.
- Select the forces to be changed.
- Look for ways of influencing these forces in the ways required.

This technique is useful particularly where human factors are important, such as in behavioural problems and changes in working practices or systems.

Mathematical models

Problems which involve quantitative information need to be represented in mathematical terms, even if it is only to

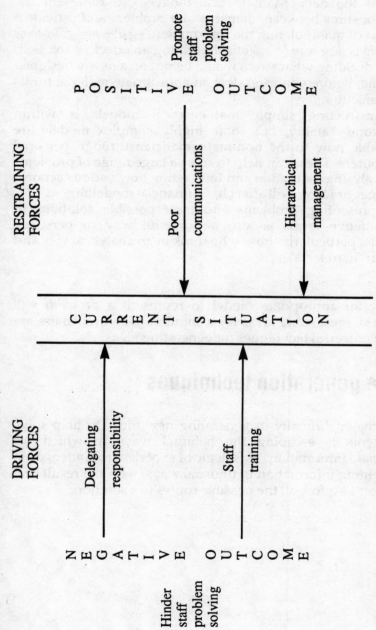

Figure 7.3 A force field diagram

record the data. Mathematical models can represent the relationships between elements of a problem and provide a means of manipulating the information, eg $a + b = c$. *In some situations they may be essential* in finding an effective solution, eg in deciding what stress would be put on a newly designed turbine, before you can select an appropriate material for its manufacture.

Constructing simple mathematical models is within everyone's ability, but some highly complex models are available now to the non-mathematician through personal computers. These can help to solve a large range of problems by analysing a situation and forecasting how various actions, changes or forces will affect it, eg financial modelling.

Representing problems and their possible solutions in quantitative terms is also a powerful way to persuade people, particularly those who think in an analytical way and favour 'hard facts'.

Using an appropriate model to represent a problem will often suggest some ideas for a solution. However, there are more powerful techniques for generating ideas.

Idea generation techniques

The major difficulty in generating new ideas to help solve problems is escaping the habitual ways in which we associate information. This 'logic of experience' hinders us in combining information in unusual ways, with the result that we don't explore all the possible routes to a solution.

ACTIVITY

Briefly describe the methods you have used to generate ideas for solving problems.

GUIDELINES

There are many different techniques which help to generate new ideas, some using mental strategies and others relying on mechanical methods. The emphasis in using them is on the quantity of ideas produced rather than the quality. This gives a large number of ideas to use in devising solutions.

An important element in using nearly all of these techniques is to *suspend judgement*, which means *avoiding any type of evaluation*. Evaluating ideas puts a brake on the imagination and inhibits the mind in making unusual and potentially useful connections. Sometimes it's easy to come up with unusual or radical ideas, for example when we know we are only 'playing'. However, as soon as we face a serious task we exclude these ideas, either consciously or unconsciously, simply because they are not commonly associated with a practical solution.

During idea generation you should try to *think in a playful way by deliberately suspending judgement* . A useful warm-up is to do a fluency exercise to get you in the right frame of mind.

Fluency exercises

Fluency is the ability to produce a large number of ideas in a short time. There are many simple, playful exercises for the imagination which can help to improve fluency. Although this improvement is not always permanent, these exercises are very useful as a warm-up for other, more productive, idea-generation techniques. In group problem solving they serve the additional purpose of overcoming individuals' reticence to voice unusual ideas.

Fluency exercises are typically simple and require you to write down as many ideas as possible in a short time, usually a minute or two. One example is to select a common object and list as many possible uses for it as you can think of in that time. Another example is to think of a bizarre situation and write down all the consequences you can think of, eg what would happen if you woke up one morning and all electrical appliances had ceased to function?

Your **flexibility of thinking** is also revealed in these exercises. The more wide-ranging your responses, the more flexible your thinking. Listing uses for newspapers, for example, you may include more common uses such as conveying news and wrapping objects, but overlook the less obvious ones such as pulping to produce bricks for burning or rolling up tightly to use as a weapon.

Fluency and flexibility usually increase with practice, so when you have a couple of minutes to relax it can be productive fun to do one of these exercises.

Free association

This technique consists of allowing the mind to wander without deliberate direction. You name the first thing that comes to mind in response to a trigger word, symbol, idea or picture, then use that as a trigger, and so on, quickly repeating the process to produce a stream of associations. The important thing is to avoid justifying the connection between successive ideas. This encourages spontaneity and the emergence of ideas seemingly unrelated to the trigger word.

Free association delves deep into the memory, helping you to discover remote relationships similar to those uncovered using mind maps. To be productive, the ideas need to be recorded, either in writing or on audio tape. This can interfere with the free flow of ideas and therefore requires practice.

Discussion

A very simple way of getting additional ideas is to discuss the problem with other people. They will often have a different perspective on the problem and its implications, and different values and ideals. Even if they can't contribute significant ideas directly, what they say may trigger new lines of thought for you. Discussing your problem with other people is a very valuable supplement to other idea generation techniques.

Daydreaming

Daydreaming is frowned upon and actively discouraged as a serious thinking skill, being labelled as fanciful, indulgent and unproductive. In fact it's one of the basic thinking tools of all good problem solvers. It has several important qualities:

- the label 'daydreaming' helps you to think in terms of time out for playful, uninhibited thinking
- it can be fitted into spare moments
- it involves only thoughts not actions, so there is no risk
- it's private, so you are not open to ridicule by others
- it often involves feelings and emotions which add a valuable dimension to your thinking
- ideas can be manipulated quickly and potential obstacles foreseen
- it helps to develop plans which prepare you to look out for information and opportunities to help you achieve objectives.

Productive daydreaming has to be directed towards a particular goal and is often called **wishful thinking**. There is no crime in wishing for the apparently impossible. Inventors do it all the time. If you set your sights high you can use daydreaming to help you build plans for achieving your goals.

Visualising

This involves thinking about a problem in visual terms. It can be useful in solving many types of problem, particularly those involving shapes and patterns. For example, if you had to devise a formula for measuring the amount of carpet required to cover a spiral staircase you would probably picture the staircase in your mind automatically. In other situations the choice may not be so obvious, but visualising is a very powerful and flexible way of thinking about problems and it can be developed with practice.

Incubation

When you get stuck with a problem after working on it for some time it's often productive to take a break from it. Once we have absorbed all the relevant information and stop work on a problem to do something else, it appears that the mind continues to manipulate the information unconsciously looking for relevant relationships and patterns. Often a new idea or even a solution will come to mind after this period of incubation.

The phrase 'sleep on it' has arisen because sleep is an enforced period of incubation. There are many reports of people awaking with new insights to a problem they have been working on. For example, Kekule is said to have discovered the ring structure of benzene after dreaming of a snake biting its tail. When time allows, putting aside a problem for a while can help in giving you a new perspective, if not a solution.

Check lists

These are *lists of thought provoking questions*. They can serve two basic purposes: to prompt the search for specific information and to stimulate ideas. Idea generation check lists work by asking what the result would be if you manipulated information in a particular way.

Check lists can be used on ideas or objects and have been developed to serve various purposes. One well known example, the 'Check List for New Ideas' developed by Alex Osborn (in *Applied Imagination*, Charles Scribner & Sons,

New York 1957), consists of a series of stimulating questions under the headings

Put to other uses?   Substitute?
Adapt?   Rearrange?
Modify?   Reverse?
Magnify?   Combine?
Minify?

Questions under the heading 'Rearrange', for example, are: Interchange components? Other patterns? Other layout? Other sequence? Transpose cause and effect? Change pace? Change schedule?

The ideal check list is one that you have designed to use in a particular situation. One simple check list, which is easy to remember and can be used as a basis for writing your own list of questions, is known by the acronym **SCAMPER**:

Substitute?
Combine?
Adapt?
Modify?
Put to other uses?
Eliminate?
Reverse?

Check lists are very flexible and, if used wisely, can be very useful when you get stuck with a problem. You can also design one consisting of prompts to help you overcome blocks you may experience in solving problems (like those described in Chapter 3).

Bug lists

This term is used by James L. Adams in his book *Conceptual Blockbusting* (W.W. Norton, New York and London 1979), to refer to a list of things which cause you, or others, irritation or dissatisfaction. It's purpose is *to stimulate the search for opportunities*.

This method can be applied usefully in organisations by soliciting the opinions of staff in terms of factors such as: What things take you more time than you think is necessary? Why? What situations cause you frustration? Why? What things do you have to do which you think are unnecessary? Why? Answers to questions such as these reveal opportunities for improving job satisfaction of staff as well as for improving efficiency.

Analogy

One of the dangers in problem solving is choosing a solution to a current problem because it has worked on a similar (analogous) problem in the past. However, analogies can provide a model which gives greater insight into a problem.

An example of how analogy can lead to innovation is the float technique of glass production. While Alastair Pilkington was washing dishes he noticed the grease floating on the water. When the float technique was perfected it consisted of molten glass floating on a bed of molten tin. Similarly, while at a wine harvest celebration the German printer Johannes Gutenberg is said to have seen the analogy between the wine press and the concept of printing.

The natural world abounds with analogies which are particularly useful in areas such as engineering and design. You can search for analogies relevant to particular problems or you may come across one by chance while you are working on a problem.

Excursions

This term is used in Synectics (see p153) to refer to techniques for distancing yourself from a problem to create a fresh perspective. It involves finding metaphors – words or phrases not directly applicable to the problem – which help to suggest solutions. These may have no practical value but they can be made to 'force-fit' the problem, ie forcing them to have some relevance. Here are two examples of excursions:

1. Take an idea from the problem definition and look for examples of it in a totally different environment. For example, if you were looking for ways to reduce the antagonism between members of a team and looked at the world of astronomy:

- Gravity pulls planets together – a grave situation might pull the team together.
- The sun 'brightens' the earth – what might brighten team members?
- A dying star disappears in an explosion – would an 'explosion' clear the air between team members?

2. Look around the room and let your gaze fall on some object. Then try to relate this to your problem. For example, you've presented a report containing inaccurate information given to you by your deputy and it has lost you an important sale. Your gaze falls on a stapler:

- 'pin' the blame on your deputy
- 'join' forces with your deputy or 'stick' your neck out to win back the sale.

This technique is not easy to use but it can bring totally new perspectives to a problem.

Paradoxes

This is another technique used in Synectics. The paradox, also known as a 'book title', is a two-word phrase, usually an adjective and noun, which captures the essence of a problem as a stimulating contradiction. For example, you have a single opportunity to meet two long-standing, valuable clients but at the same time and in different locations. Both meetings are vitally important in their own way. Useful paradoxes might be

- attentive neglect – you will have to neglect one client but want to appear attentive

- disloyal allegiance – you want to avoid appearing disloyal to the client you don't meet
- singular double – you are only one person but need to be two.

Paradoxes, like excursions, help to create new perspectives and suggest new routes to a solution.

Forced relationships

This simple technique combines unrelated objects or ideas to see what new, practical combinations result. There are many products on the market which are the result of such a combination, eg the digital wrist watch which includes a stopwatch and calculator; televisions with a newspaper-type information service, like Oracle and Prestel; the Swiss Army knife; the combined washing machine and tumble dryer; birthday cards which play a musical tune.

Attribute listing

This is an analytical technique used *to identify ways in which a product, service or system could be improved*. It consists of three stages:

- the physical attributes or characteristics of each component of the item are described
- the functions of each component are described
- every component is examined in turn to see if changing its physical attributes would bring about an improvement in its function.

A simple example would be the screwdriver, which has numerous improved variations, including a filament for current detection, multiple screw-in shafts, magnetic blades and ratchet mechanisms.

Attribute listing can also be used to search for alternative areas in which a product or service could be used, by looking for applications for individual attributes. The attributes of optical fibres, for instance, have made them useful in fields as diverse as telecommunications, medicine and exhibition lighting.

Another use of attribute listing is in *value analysis*. This involves looking at the cost of each component of the item in relation to the function it performs. Components which are disproportionately costly in relation to their function can be either eliminated or ways found to reduce their cost. The aim is to increase the ratio of value against cost.

A fourth application is in *analysing systems to find areas of potential improvement*. For example, listing the attributes of data processing functions within an organisation may reveal two areas which require the same or a similar resource but which are currently served by separate systems. Serving both needs by one resource may result in cost savings. Another example is where the attributes of a waste product are used to search for ways in which it might be used as a raw material for another product or a new product, possibly using some parts of the existing production system.

Morphological analysis

This term refers to a variety of techniques which are similar to forced relationships and attribute listing. They can be applied to ideas, problems, objects or systems, which are broken down into their individual components so that every possible combination can be searched for something new and practical.

Although there are several variations, a simple method involves the following stages: the parameters of the situation are listed; each one is subdivided into its smallest parts; these are represented in a matrix; then all possible combinations are examined.

There are a variety of ways to represent this information. Cards or sheets of paper can be used to list each component, either individually or grouped under headings, and then shuffled to create various combinations. Alternatively, the information can be grouped and written on the outer edge of different sized circles of card, which are pinned together

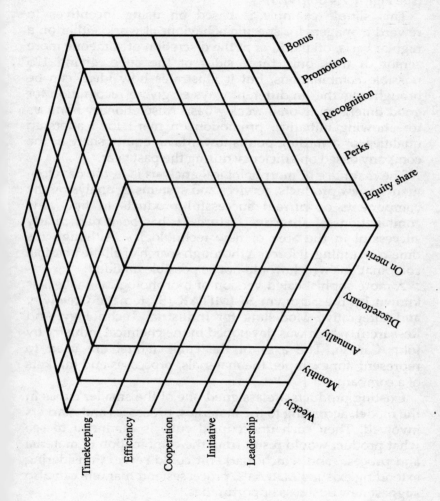

fig 7.4

through the centre and rotated to bring different components together. Perhaps the easiest method is to draw a three-dimensional cube divided into many smaller cubes (see Figure 7.4 on p141).

This simple example is based on using incentives to reward managers for specific behaviour at work, either on a regular basis, on merit, or at the discretion of someone more senior. It uses only three sides of the cube, giving 125 possible combinations, but it illustrates how ideas can be brought together in different ways eg giving recognition for good timekeeping on a weekly basis, discretionary bonuses for showing initiative, promotion on merit for leadership qualities, or awarding points towards an equity share in the company based on efficiency during the past year.

The main use of morphological analysis is in the development of new products, services and systems eg analysing the components of current successful products to find new combinations of attractive features. It has been particularly successful in the area of new technologies. Although it's time-consuming, it forces a thorough search of all the possible combinations which would not be possible unaided.

A more sophisticated version of morphological analysis is known by the acronym **SCIMITAR** (Systematic Creativity and Integrative Modelling for Industrial Technology And Research), which was developed in the chemical industry by John Carson. The axes of the cubic model are used to represent, for example, the materials, processes and markets of a company.

Existing products are assigned one of the smaller cubes in the model, according to the materials, processes and markets involved. Then each unoccupied cube is examined to see what product would result from the combination of material and process, and which market it could serve. Considering extending existing materials, processes and markets can also suggest new business opportunities.

Deciding which type of model and idea generation technique it is best to use is often determined by the type of problem you are tackling and what you are trying to achieve. In situations where you have a choice of several methods, practice will tell you which ones work best for you.

Although some of the techniques may appear cumbersome and time-consuming, with practice you will find that they become less mechanical as the styles of thinking they encourage become incorporated into your natural problem solving style.

KEY
POINTS

- The human mind cannot hold a complete picture of a complex problem, so it's often difficult to see all the relationships involved.
- Creating a model of a problem helps to clarify the relationships between its different parts.
- We develop habitual ways of looking at situations which prevents us seeing beyond the obvious.
- There are many techniques to help break these habits, creating new ideas in the search for solutions.

PROJECT

Select two different problems that you have faced in the past or are facing now and apply one of the techniques described in this chapter to each of them.

Chapter 8

Solving problems in a group

A large amount of problem solving takes place in group settings. Meetings and informal discussions are often used to air different ideas and points of view to help solve problems for which the participants have either shared responsibility or a contribution to make. However, most of the time we do not take full advantage of these situations.

Used at the right time and in the right way, group problem solving can be the most effective way of solving some problems. This chapter will help you to

- recognise when group problem solving offers the best chance of finding an effective solution
- avoid pitfalls and get the best out of the group
- learn how to use specific techniques for solving problems in a group.

When to use group problem solving

Although there are very definite advantages to solving certain problems as a group, others can be solved more effectively by an individual. It's important to know when and when not to work in a group.

Use this checklist to decide when to use group problem solving:

- Can the problem be defined in many different ways?
- Is information from many different sources required?
- Is it a very specialised problem, where the 'expert' might be biased or not see the wider implications?
- Does the problem have implications for many people?
- Are there likely to be many possible solutions?
- Is it a complex problem with many different aspects?
- Will a solution need to be agreed by others before it can be implemented?

The more questions you answer 'yes', the more appropriate it is to use group problem solving. However, the deciding question is always: 'Are suitable and relevant people available to work together in solving this problem?'

Getting the best out of group problem solving

Problem solving is a complex and at times frustrating process. It requires a careful manipulation of mental strategies which is very susceptible to outside influence.

ACTIVITY

Think about what is involved in solving problems and compare that with what typically happens in meetings, especially reactions to each other's ideas. Bearing this in mind, list what you think are the advantages and disadvantages of solving problems in a group.

ADVANTAGES	DISADVANTAGES

GUIDELINES

When people are working together it's inevitable that they will be influenced by each other. This can have a significant effect on the efficiency of group problem solving.

The **disadvantages** of group problem solving can include:

Competition

Most people working in a group unconsciously perceive the situation as competitive. This generates behaviour which is destructive and drains the creative energy of the group. For example, we often perceive disagreement with our ideas as a put-down. The natural reaction is to try to regain our self-esteem, often by trying to sabotage the ideas of those who disagreed with us. Instead of looking for ways to improve on their ideas we choose to destroy them.

Eager to express our own ideas, we may totally ignore what others are suggesting. Power-seekers may use ploys such as highlighting flaws in others' arguments, barbed questions and displays of expertise to show their supremacy. These types of behaviour create an atmosphere which is incompatible with effective problem solving.

Conformity

There is a strong tendency for individuals in a group to want to conform to the consensus. This can be for a variety of reasons, including the need to feel liked, valued or respected, and tends to make people censor their ideas accordingly. The comparative status of the individuals present also has an important influence. Senior members often want to maintain their image of being knowledgeable, while junior members want to avoid appearing the inexperienced 'upstart'. Because agreement on ideas can be gained quickly in a group setting, groups tend to select and approve solutions quickly, without exploring all the possibilities.

Lack of objective direction

Most traditional meetings and group discussions convened to solve problems are ineffectively directed. Sometimes there is no effective leader to give direction to the discussion, with the result that it wanders aimlessly. Even when there is strong leadership, the group leader or chairman often exerts undue pressure on the direction and content of the discussion. In addition, the ideas aired during a meeting are not usually recorded, apart from the minutes and individual note-taking, with the result that many ideas are forgotten and cannot act as a constant stimulus to the discussion.

Time constraints

Group problem solving is a relatively slow process compared with working alone. It requires individuals to come together at an agreed time, usually for about one hour, and this can cause organisational problems as well as impatience amongst participants to 'get it over with' as quickly as possible.

The **advantages** of group problem solving can include:

Greater output

Simply because of the number of people involved, each with differing experience, knowledge, points of view and values, a larger number and variety of ideas for solving a problem can be produced.

Cross fertilisation

The exchange of ideas can act as a stimulus to the imagination, encouraging individuals to explore ideas they would not otherwise consider.

Reduced bias

The shared responsibility of a group in arriving at decisions can encourage individuals to explore seemingly unrealistic ideas and to challenge accepted ways of doing things. Individual biases and prejudices can be challenged by the group, forcing the individual to recognise them. Group pressure can also encourage individuals to accept that change is needed.

Increased risk taking

Shared responsibility makes individuals more willing to take risks. The discussion of different points of view also helps the group to be more realistic in assessing the risks associated with particular courses of action.

Higher commitment

When goals are agreed it gives a common purpose to the group, within which individuals can gain a feeling of self-determination and recognition through their contribution. Individuals who have contributed to finding a solution feel a greater commitment to its successful implementation.

Improved communication

When people who are affected by a problem or who will be involved in implementation are involved in finding a solution, they will know how and why that particular solution was chosen. Also, people with knowledge relevant to the problem can communicate that knowledge directly if they participate in solving the problem.

Better solutions

Groups of individuals can bring a broad range of ideas, knowledge and skills to bear on a problem. This creates a stimulating interaction of diverse ideas which results in a wider range and better quality of solutions.

ACTIVITY

Briefly describe how, in a group, you could achieve the following:

Maximise the freedom to express unusual and radical ideas.

Encourage a large number and wide range of ideas.

Give direction to the contributions.

GUIDELINES

The primary reason why group problem solving can be less effective than the individual problem solver is that *a group effort needs to be managed skilfully*. Various techniques have been developed to capitalise on the strengths of group problem solving and to avoid its potential weaknesses. These define the role of the participants, including the leader, and the methods used by the group.

Participants should be selected to give the group a diversity of experience in various disciplines. Not all of them should be familiar with the problem area under consideration because these people may be too close to see it in perspective and may be biased towards conventional solutions. People with little or no relevant experience bring a new perspective and are more likely to think of unusual solutions.

All participants should understand the function of the group and what is expected of them. A mix of sexes, of quiet and lively personalities, and of ages creates a stimulating interaction. The mixing of widely differing ranks should be avoided, especially in organisations where staff are conscious of status. Individuals can be inhibited in expressing unusual ideas by the presence of higher or lower ranking people than themselves.

The **methods** used, which are described later in this chapter, are designed to stimulate creativity and to give coherent direction to the individual contributions. They help to remove the pressures and constraints which exist in a normal meeting and to create an atmosphere and frame of mind conducive to creative problem solving. The *group leader plays a key role* in creating the right kind of atmosphere and prompting individuals in their search for solutions.

Leadership of group problem solving is different to the traditional role of the chairman of a meeting. The chair normally decides what issues are to be discussed and judges what comments are relevant and what areas are worth exploring. The leader in group problem solving is there primarily to stimulate and record ideas from the other participants. The precise role varies slightly in the different group techniques, but basically it includes

- briefing participants
- keeping contributions flowing at a fast pace
- ensuring that everyone contributes
- clarifying ideas when necessary
- ensuring that everyone sticks to the 'rules'
- not allowing anyone to be put on the defensive
- prompting individuals to build on each other's ideas
- prompting the group to explore new avenues
- ensuring that the quiet and less experienced individuals are given a chance to air their ideas
- recording and displaying the group's ideas.

The *primary function of the leader* is not to allow any participant to be put on the defensive, so that they can concentrate on thinking up ideas rather than defending them. During idea generation anyone who judges or criticises ideas – through words, tone or gesture – is told forcefully by the leader to '*suspend judgement*'. The purpose is to avoid excluding impractical or seemingly ridiculous ideas which later could be developed into something useful. A good knowledge of the mechanics of the particular technique, an infectious enthusiasm and a good sense of humour are ideal characteristics for a leader.

Techniques for group problem solving

The two major group techniques designed specifically for problem solving are brainstorming and Synectics. Quality circles are primarily concerned with problem solving but serve additional, broader functions.

Brainstorming and Synectics use a common method for

giving direction to the problem solving activity. First, the problem is defined in terms of 'How to ...?'. This wording has the advantage that it doesn't have to be a realistic statement of what the group wants to achieve, so it doesn't need to be justified and impractical ideas are not discouraged. Then solutions to these problem definitions are sought in response to the question 'In how many ways can we ...?'. This takes the group from formulating goals to suggesting ways to achieve them. Both group techniques also help to stimulate the imagination of participants by displaying prominently all the ideas as they are produced.

Brainstorming

The technique of brainstorming, which was devised in an advertising agency, is *designed to generate a large number and range of ideas in a short time*. This is achieved by concentrating solely on idea generation and creating a light-hearted, free-wheeling atmosphere.

The number of people in a brainstorming session varies between 5 and 20, with an optimum of about 12. Everyone present contributes ideas, including the leader, because non-participating observers can have an inhibiting effect. Sessions are held in a room away from distractions, with chairs arranged in a U-shape and a flipchart with something like newsprint which can be used to record ideas and then torn off and pinned to the walls. Sessions can last anything up to 2 hours, although the longer they are the more difficult it is to sustain the flow of ideas. The finishing time should be left open so that it does not curtail a fruitful session.

The leader's role begins with preparation for the session, gaining a full understanding of the problem and selecting and inviting participants who are given a brief description of the problem. During the session the leader contributes, stimulates and records ideas. Constant structured stimulation is needed to keep the ideas flowing and everyone participating.

There are **four basic rules** to be followed in a brainstorming session and it is the leader's job to enforce them:

Suspend judgement

No evaluation is allowed during the session and the leader must be able to enforce this rule even with very high ranking individuals.

Free-wheel

This is the lowering of barriers and inhibitions about what is practical and impractical so that the mind can wander freely. It is encouraged by the 'suspend judgement' rule and by humour and laughter in response to silly ideas.

Cross-fertilise

Participants are encouraged to modify and develop other people's ideas and to express any further ideas these suggest.

Quantity

Participants are encouraged to produce a large number of ideas irrespective of whether they are practical or impractical. A good session can produce hundreds of ideas.

All energy in a brainstorming session is directed towards producing ideas for solving the problem. Evaluation of the group's ideas is not a part of the session, which involves the following stages:

- defining and discussing the problem
- restating the problem
- warming up
- brainstorming.

Defining and discussing the problem

The problem is described briefly by someone with knowledge of the situation, giving enough information for the others to understand it but not enough to inhibit their ideas for a solution. This stage usually takes around five minutes.

Restating the problem

Group members restate the problem, looking at it from different angles and phrasing it in terms of 'How to ...?'. The leader writes these down on newsprint. Throughout the session all ideas are numbered serially to make them easier to identify later. Restatement continues until all ideas are exhausted. This should result in at least 25 restatements, often many more.

Warming up

At this stage it is useful to use one of the fluency exercises described in Chapter 7, such as 'other uses for ...' and the consequences of bizarre situations. This helps to get the group members in a free-wheeling frame of mind. None of these ideas are recorded.

Brainstorming

One of the restatements is selected either by voting or by the leader, who then writes it down on a new sheet of paper beginning with the words 'In how many ways can we ...?'. The leader reads the restatement and asks for ideas, writing them down as they are called out. When a sheet is full it is displayed prominently on the wall to act as a stimulus to further ideas. When all the ideas have been exhausted another restatement is selected, as remote as possible from the first one, and the process is repeated. Three or four restatements are treated in this way.

There are various things the leader can do to stimulate the group, including repeating ideas as they are written down, asking for variations on an earlier idea, and calling for another warming up exercise. The leader can also suggest ideas which lead the group into new areas. When ideas dry up the leader asks the group to select the **wildest idea** from the lists and to suggest useful variations. A couple of the wildest ideas are treated in this way before the leader ends the session with a description of the evaluation process.

Evaluation starts a few days after the brainstorming session, once a list of all the ideas produced has been typed. There are two methods of evaluation – by a small team of people selected from the original session, including the leader and others committed to solving the problem, and by all the participants individually. Using both methods helps to prevent potentially useful ideas being discarded.

The list of ideas produced is sent to individual participants who are asked to select a small proportion of the ideas that they feel could be useful in solving the problem. They send the numbers of these ideas to the leader, who collates them and discards ideas which received few votes. The team also meets to discuss the full list of ideas, using criteria of effectiveness first to weed out the impractical ideas and then to select the best ones.

The two lists of remaining ideas are collated by the leader and the highest voting ideas selected for further evaluation. At this stage the ideas are examined to see how they could be modified and improved before they are rejected or accepted. Various creative techniques described in Chapter 7 can be used for this purpose.

Under some circumstances, *brainstorming sessions can be conducted successfully in a less structured way.* One particular application is in the creation of brand names. Starting with a product description, under the direction of the leader, group members explore all the associations that a product might inspire in the mind of the consumer. Visual images of the various lifestyles associated with the product can be used to help stimulate ideas for names.

A two hour session, with several products under consideration, may generate around 2000 names. Later these are screened carefully, throwing out those names already in use and checking by linguists to ensure that translation into different languages would not create a disastrous association with the product.

Synectics

The major differences with Synectics are that it combines short periods (5–10 minutes) of controlled analysis and creative idea generation, it aims to arrive at a solution in less than an hour, and the leader is not allowed to contribute ideas.

A Synectics group consists of the problem owner, a leader and 5–8 participants, and is held in a room equipped like that used in brainstorming. The session seeks to create a solution acceptable to the **problem owner**, who has the power to decide which avenues are to be explored further and which are rejected. The overall purpose is to get commitment from the problem owner to implement the solution, so the **participants** need to be good listeners in order to understand and build on the ideas that the problem owner favours. The **leader** guides the session and stimulates and records the ideas of the group.

ACTIVITY

Write down five questions or comments that the leader in a brainstorming or Synectics session could use to encourage contributions without narrowing the potential responses.

GUIDELINES

The leader can make a wide range of non-limiting, prompting comments, eg

- Tell me ways in which we could achieve that.
- Any ideas?
- Can we build on this?
- Can we do that in a different way?
- What would be the ideal?
- Let's have some really wild ideas.
- Who cares – let's just play with the idea.
- Can you tell me more about that?

In Synectics, where there are periods of analysis and evaluation, at times the leader also uses prompting comments such as

- Where could that idea be improved?
- What's useful about this?
- What are your worries about this?

In brainstorming prompts for criticism must not be given and in Synectics they must only be used at the appropriate phase of the session.

A Synectics session can be divided broadly into six stages:

Problem as given
The problem owner states the problem in one sentence, phrased in terms of 'How to ...?' or 'How can I ...?'. This is written down as given.

Analysis
The problem owner gives brief background information on the problem, including

- what the problem is
- how it has arisen
- why it's a problem
- what solutions have been suggested or tried and rejected
- why these were ineffective or insufficient
- what power the problem owner has to implement a solution
- what the ideal solution would be, in terms of 'It would be nice if ...'.

This briefing should stimulate the imagination of the group through the emotional tone and the use of rich, evocative language. During this stage the participants make notes on ideas which occur to them for solution, alternative ways of seeing the problem, and so on. Together, these first two stages should take only about five minutes.

Restatement
The participants and owner restate the problem in terms of 'How to ...?' and comment briefly on their reasons, while the leader writes them down. No evaluation is allowed at this stage, which should produce at least 20 restatements and take no more than ten minutes.

Selection
The problem owner selects one or two of the restatements which appear useful, explaining briefly why and how they should be developed. Participants continue to make notes on ideas that come to mind.

Solution development
The group suggest a few possible solutions and may build on each other's ideas. The problem owner paraphrases these to ensure that they've been understood. The leader then asks the owner to select one solution and to explain briefly a couple of its major attractions and its major drawback. This drawback is stated in terms of 'How to ...?'. The group then suggests a few ideas for overcoming this drawback from

which the owner selects one, again explaining a couple of the attractions and the major drawback. This process is repeated until the owner accepts the solution or until the end of the session is reached.

The group concentrates on building on the positive aspects of solutions while overcoming the problem owner's reservations about them. This encourages movement towards a solution rather than a stalemate created by competition and defensiveness. Various creative techniques, including word association, analogies, excursions and paradoxes, are introduced by the leader to help the group to explore all possible routes to a solution. These techniques are described in Chapter 7.

Possible solution

This is the final stage, where the problem owner explains the attractions of the solution and the steps that will be taken to implement it. This commitment to act when a feasible solution has been found is important to the morale of the group.

An example of Synectics in use is when Kimberly-Clark was looking for ways to reduce the distribution costs for Kleenex tissues. The solution chosen was to compress the tissues to remove excess air, resulting in a smaller box. This required fewer materials and warehouse space, reduced the transport costs, and had possible advantages in terms of point of sale display and product appeal to consumers.

Synectics and brainstorming have different merits. Synectics can lead to a solution in a short time but gives less scope for generating a wide range of possible solutions, while brainstorming, which takes much longer when evaluation is included, produces a large number of ideas and possible solutions.

Quality circles

Quality circles have a broader function than brainstorming and Synectics and therefore are not so narrowly structured and controlled. Although their activities are directed at problem solving *to improve the quality of the company's products and services and reduce costs,* they produce other benefits such as increased staff awareness of quality, greater job satisfaction, improved motivation, better communications and better utilisation of the intellectual skills of the workforce.

Quality circles consist of around 4–12 people from the same work area who meet voluntarily on a regular basis to solve their work-related problems. Typically meetings are held weekly, fortnightly or monthly and range in length from 1–2 hours. They are held in paid time and a room is usually set aside for the sole use of the circle, equipped with noticeboards, flipcharts, audio visual equipment, and so on. The circle leader is often the supervisor of the work group involved and usually has been on a short off-the-job training course. Circle members contribute ideas on problem areas to be tackled and invite suggestions from others outside the group, voting to decide which problem they will tackle first.

Information needed to solve the problem is collected by the group, including management information relating to the problem such as the cost of an existing process or the manufacturing costs of a product. Various creative techniques are used to suggest a range of possible solutions, including *brainstorming* and *force field analysis*. The circle evaluates solutions in terms of their effectiveness, their effects on other departments, the costs and savings to the company, and the likelihood of their acceptance by management.

When a solution has been selected it is presented at a meeting with the relevant management. This presentation is often rehearsed and includes a description of the problem, an explanation of why it was considered a problem, what the recommended solution is and what its benefits are, and an outline of what action is required to implement the solution. When practical, *the circle members are also involved in the implementation of the solution.* Usually there is no financial reward for ideas, although in some companies the ideas can be put into the suggestion scheme which may result in financial reward.

Communication between members of the quality circle and

the rest of the workforce is extremely important. As well as inviting ideas on problems to be tackled, the circle reports back on its activities. *Maintaining a high visibility for the circle is important to meet many of its objectives.*

Setting up and running a quality circle programme requires planning and management. A management committee, usually made up of representatives of various rank from different departments, initiates the programme and makes decisions on its development, the methods for selecting leaders and members, how they will operate, and the evaluation policy. A facilitator or coordinator deals with the day-to-day running of the quality circles.

Unless your company operates a quality circle programme, or you are in a position to initiate one, this method is not accessible to you, although you may like to find out why it is not being used in your organisation. The choice between brainstorming and Synectics depends on various factors, such as the urgency of the problem, the availability of a skilled leader, and personal preferences.

KEY
POINTS

- Not all problems are solved more effectively by a group, so the reasons for choosing a group method must be identified.
- To be effective, group problem solving has to be managed skillfully.
- There are a number of group problem solving methods, including brainstorming, Synectics and quality circles, each with specific advantages.

PROJECT

If you have never participated in a brainstorming session, try to arrange a session with colleagues or friends to tackle a problem which concerns you all. Try to involve someone with experience of brainstorming and follow the outline given in this chapter.

Alternatively , if you have participated in a brainstorming or Synectics session, answer the following questions:

Was there effective group leadership?

In what ways could the group's performance have been improved?

Chapter 9

Evaluating your solutions

When you have more than one possible solution to a problem, each involving a different course of action with different advantages and disadvantages, you need to evaluate these to decide which will be the most effective in achieving your objective. Even when you have only one solution you still need to decide whether it is acceptable and make the decision to implement it. This chapter will help you to

- understand clearly what evaluating the options involves
- learn appropriate evaluation techniques.

What evaluation involves

Deciding which of your solutions will provide the most acceptable means of achieving your objective is a complex process of decision making. Your ultimate choice is often a compromise between conflicting needs and between the benefits and disadvantages of each solution.

ACTIVITY

Try to recall a situation where you decided upon a particular course of action which turned out to be unsuccessful. List the reasons for making this decision badly. Alternatively, list the reasons bad decisions are made.

GUIDELINES

There are many ways in which you can arrive at a bad decision, including

- not having sufficient alternatives from which to choose
- not considering all the alternatives
- lack of time
- lack of information
- not being methodical
- inaccurate forecasting of the effects of specific actions
- inaccurate forecasting of external influences
- hazy objectives
- ignorance of evaluation techniques
- uncritical acceptance of others' judgements
- poor work at an earlier stage of problem solving
- uncritical acceptance of subjective needs and feelings
- an impulsive response.

A good decision is one based on a methodical evaluation of all the options against the exact requirements of the objective, taking into account any obstacles, the constraints of the situation and the risks involved.

Who should be involved?

There are many situations where a manager can choose a solution and issue instructions for it to be implemented without involving anyone else in the decision-making process. Sometimes you may wish to consult others out of regard for them personally or because it is politic. At other times it may be essential to involve others, eg

- when you have a formal obligation to consult others
- when you require additional information
- when expert skills are required to evaluate the options
- when you need the commitment of others for the solution to be implemented successfully.

Formal obligation

Sometimes you are obliged to consult others because of the nature of the decision, eg when it involves actions beyond your authority.

Information

To be able to evaluate solutions effectively you often need additional information, eg about what would be a satisfactory solution, what value should be placed on the different results that your various solutions would achieve, or what resources are available to implement a solution.

Skills

Sometimes evaluating solutions will require expert skills in a particular discipline eg predicting the consequences of new tax legislation, the analysis of a particular market, or forecasting the reaction of staff to a new working practice.

Commitment

When a problem or its solution involves other people, individually or as a group, it's often necessary to gain their commitment to the solution. This may be essential in certain situations, such as when it requires them to use their initiative and skills to make it work, or when it is common practice (eg decisions affecting union members). You may need the commitment of

- those involved with the problem and the solution (eg staff, customers, clients, suppliers)
- those who have to agree to the solution
- those who will provide the necessary resources

- those who have to implement the solution.

One way of gaining commitment is to involve people in the decision making process. Answering the following questions will help you to decide which of the people you have identified in the groups above need to be involved:

- Why do I need their commitment to the solution?
- Can I gain their commitment without involving them in decision making? (eg offer them persuasive benefits, use my authority)
- Do those I need to involve have a common view of the purpose of this decision? (If not, there could be conflicting interests at work and it may be better to look for another way of encouraging their commitment.)

You can involve other people either individually or collectively. When you seek help, advice and opinions on a one-to-one basis you usually retain overall responsibility for making the decision. In a group you can either retain the option to veto the group's decision or take part as an equal member and agree to accept the collective decision. Group decision making has the advantage that responsibility is shared and individual subjective bias and prejudice is reduced.

Most of us have a natural reluctance to change our mind once we have made a decision, even when we realise that it's not the best decision under the circumstances. When you change your mind it can feel sometimes like admitting to a fault in making the wrong decision in the first place, or that your authority is being undermined. Usually we can think of many reasons for not changing our mind and many 'rational' ways to justify our initial choice. *It's much easier to make the right decision first time than to change your mind later.*

In some situations, such as deciding how to spend your annual leave, your decision may be heavily influenced by subjective values. Sometimes you may have to make a snap decision and need to rely upon past experience of similar situations and upon your intuition. However, personal preferences and biases can mislead in situations where an objective decision is required. In general, therefore, *decisions should be based on a logical and objective evaluation of all the options*, even though the subjective opinions of all those involved need to be considered.

Evaluating the solutions

There are various ways of evaluating the possible solutions to a problem but basically you need to identify and compare their relative values. This information must be recorded and presented in a meaningful way to aid comparison. It can also be used to persuade other people to accept the decision and help to communicate the solution to those involved in its implementation. **Decision trees** are one way of representing the various choices that need to be made in deciding which is the most effective course of action (see chain diagrams in Chapter 7).

The evaluation process can be divided into six stages:

- defining the 'ideal' solution
- eliminating unviable solutions, ie those which do not meet the constraints
- evaluating the remaining solutions against the results required
- assessing the risks associated with the 'best' solution and, if acceptable
- making the decision.

Defining the ideal solution

The criteria of effectiveness which you defined to guide your search for solutions are inadequate to make an effective evaluation. Each solution may differ slightly or radically in the way and the extent to which it achieves your various goals. To be able to evaluate these effectively you need to *construct a model of the 'ideal' solution* against which to measure them.

ACTIVITY

List the factors you would include in constructing a model of
an ideal solution.

GUIDELINES

To define the ideal solution you need to consider the results required and the constraints that have to be met. The **results required** include the benefits desired in terms of the objective, dealing effectively with obstacles/causes, and sometimes acceptance of the solution (and/or its effects) by other people.

Depending on your objective, the **benefits desired** may be fixed, such as restarting a halted production line, or flexible, such as achieving the highest possible market share (although there may be constraints in terms of the lowest acceptable market share/cost ratio).

When achieving the desired results means that you must have dealt with **obstacles/causes** effectively, these can be omitted from your list of required results, eg if you succeed in introducing a new working practice it means that you will have overcome possible resistance from employees. Other situations may not be so clear-cut and then you need to define what it means to deal with obstacles/causes effectively, eg to improve the service you offer customers you may need to analyse their perceptions of your current service and this could involve overcoming barriers to communication between you.

When **acceptance of the solution** by other people is essential you need to list the factors which will make it acceptable to them, eg not increasing their workload, or not decreasing their authority.

Constraints are generally specified as the limits of resources (time, space, money, materials and manpower), the mimimum results that will be acceptable and the maximum disadvantages that can be tolerated.

Resources may be limited by what is available or what the problem justifies.

The **minimum results** that you will accept may be stated in absolute terms, such as achieving 100% accuracy in quality control, or in relative terms, such as achieving 100% accuracy provided it does not cost over £18,000 per annum. The **maximum disadvantages** which can be tolerated are stated in terms of unacceptable cost in resources and undesirable side-effects.

Other factors may also represent a constraint, eg company policy (perhaps dictating how certain issues are handled) and legislation (such as local planning restrictions).

Here is a simple example of what an ideal solution might look like.

Problem:
Reduce expenditure on stationery from £1850 per month to under £1500 per month within 6 months.

Results required:
- expenditure on stationery under £1500 per month (a 20% reduction)
- wastage, misuse and pilfering of stationery prevented
- a simple administrative system

Constraints:
- target to be achieved within 6 months
- no additional administrative time beyond the current level to be necessary once the target has been achieved
- supplier cannot be changed (for political reasons)
- a 15% reduction in costs would be acceptable initially
- a blatant 'policing' strategy will not be acceptable

There would be many different ways of achieving this ideal solution, each providing different benefits and disadvantages. One solution might achieve a saving by distributing stationery regularly on a controlled basis, but run the risk of sometimes leaving people without essential items. Another solution might be to make people accountable for their stationery costs, but this could be viewed as petty and involve extra paperwork, putting an additional burden on already over-worked staff.

It's often difficult to choose between solutions which have different disadvantages and which provide the results required in different amounts. For example, would it be better to prevent wastage of stationery completely even if it required complex administration, or to accept reduced wastage using a simpler system? To deal with this type of situation *you need to give points to each result required according to its relative value*. This is done by selecting the most important result, giving it an arbitrary value (eg 5), and then rating all the other results against this standard. Disadvantages are given negative values according to their relative severity.

Deciding the relative values of the results required and the disadvantages of various solutions can be a difficult task and may require discussion with others involved with the problem to ensure that the values are objective.

Decisions are not always made by choosing the optimum mix of all the criteria of effectiveness. Instead the following strategies may be used in certain situations:

Satisficing refers to the selection of any solution which achieves a minimum set of requirements. It could be used when there is insufficient time for a detailed evaluation of all the options or insufficient information for a full evaluation.

Maximising refers to giving preference to one particular evaluation criterion eg employ the individual with the best telephone manner. This could be used when one criterion has a particular siginificance and when there is insufficient time or information for a full evaluation.

Minimising refers to giving preference to solutions with minimal disadvantage on a particular criterion eg. buy the make of popular car which shows minimum depreciation.

Check your ideal solution before using it to evaluate solutions by answering following questions.

- Is it an accurate reflection of what would be ideal under the circumstances?
- Does it take account of the needs of all the people involved?
- Are there any conflicting or inconsistent results required?
- Are the relative values you have given the criteria free from bias or other distortions?
- Do they conform to departmental and organisational policies?

When the outcome of a particular course of action is uncertain you need to estimate the probabilities of what will happen. In trying to find 80 new dealers to stock one of your products, for example, you may have considered, amongst other approaches, direct mail and personal visits by sales staff. To evaluate these two courses of action you would need to estimate the conversion rate for each, ie the probability of a new dealer being recruited per visit and per mail piece.

Probability is expressed as a figure between 0 and 1, where 0 is no probability and 1 is complete certainty. The probability of finding a new dealer through a mail shot, for example, may be 0.01 (1% or 1 new dealer for each 100 mailed) and through a personal visit 0.14 (14% or 14 new dealers per 100 visits). Probabilities also need to be calculated where costs and side-effects are uncertain.

You are now ready to begin evaluating your solutions. The method described below is intended to reduce the amount of time required for evaluation by first eliminating solutions which do not meet the constraints.

Eliminating unviable solutions

At this stage you examine each solution in turn and reject those which do not meet all the constraints you have identified, recording the reasons so that you can check them later. Sometimes it's possible to modify an otherwise unacceptable solution so that it does meet the constraints and can be evaluated with the others at the next stage.

POSSIBLE SOLUTIONS	RESULTS REQUIRED						DISADVANTAGES (−)		OVERALL VALUE
	Regain lost customers (4)		Attract new customers (4)		Create regular customer base (5)				
Improve food	5	20	4	16	5	25	Cost of better produce	−3	58
Improve service	5	20	5	20	5	25	Retrain staff	−1	64
Change menu regularly	3	12	5	20	4	20	Careful planning required	−1	51
Extend opening hours	3	12	4	16	4	20	Increased overheads	−3	45
Create mailing list	2	8	0	0	5	25	Intrusive	−1	32

Fig 9.1

Evaluating the remaining solutions

Each of the remaining solutions is now examined to see how well it provides the results required. The best fit on each dimension of the results is given an arbitrary value (eg 5) and the others are valued relative to this standard. As each solution is evaluated it can be represented on a chart (Figure 9.1).

This is an extract from an evaluation of ways to reverse the fall in trade of a restaurant. Redecoration and press advertising have been rejected because of cost constraints.

Each solution is composed of a variety of strategies. Improving the food, for example, may involve changing the chef, improving the quality of produce used, or improving kitchen facilities, depending on the current situation. Each alternative will have different advantages and disadvantages which need to be taken into account, eg changing the chef is unacceptable because he has a major financial stake in the restaurant and doesn't want to leave. The probability of different outcomes also may be important, such as the likely response to mail shots once a mailing list has been created.

The value of each solution in relation to each result is found by multiplying its relative value by the relative fit. The 'best' solution is the one with the highest aggregate score (ie the sum of the value of the results provided less the negative value of the disadvantages).

From the example above you can see that improving the service at the restaurant is most likely to reverse the fall in trade, followed closely by improving the food. This does not mean that these solutions have a similar effect on individual customers, but overall they are likely to produce similar results in terms of the objective. The two solutions in combination may exceed the results required but may also exceed constraints, eg the combined costs of better produce and retraining staff.

Before moving to the next stage you should check your evaluation to ensure that it's accurate and that no relevant factors have been forgotten.

Assessing the Risks

Although the solution you have chosen offers the best balance of benefits versus disadvantages, you need to examine the possible risks associated with this solution to ensure that they are acceptable and to identify areas where risks could be minimised.

ACTIVITY

Make a list of the factors that you may need to consider in
assessing the risks associated with a particular solution.

GUIDELINES

To assess the risks associated with a particular solution you need to answer the question, 'What could go wrong, how likely is it to happen and how severe would the effects be?'. There are *specific areas where risks are most likely to arise*.

Information used in the construction and evaluation of the solution. If any of this information was inaccurate it could make the solution or your evaluation of it unreliable. You need to answer questions such as:

- is there information which was key to the construction or evaluation of this solution?
- is this information reliable? (think about the source – eg could it be biased in any way? – and the method of collection)
- have any assumptions been made?
- is this an area where we have no experience or knowledge of the likely outcome?

If you suspect that any information you have used may be unrealiable you should double-check. If your suspicions are confirmed you must decide what implications they have for the likely success of the solution. For example, if a company has been highly over-optimistic in predicting that it could sell 80% of the extra goods it can produce by buying new plant, is the purchase still viable bearing in mind the reduced income from sales?

Implementation is a time when, because of its nature, the solution may become unreliable. You need to answer the question, 'What could happen if the implementation of this solution does not go as planned?', eg

- Is there sufficient leeway in meeting constraints and the results required? (eg If it takes 5% extra time to implement this solution will we still meet the deadline? If there is a price increase in this raw material will we exceed our budget?)

- Are the resources required of such magnitude or do they extend over such a prolonged period that it will leave us vulnerable? (eg If all the available incoming cash over the next eight months is committed to this expansion programme, what will happen if someone launches a competitive service and our market share falls dramatically and reduces our income?)
- If we don't keep to this time schedule could it mean that the resources required at some stage of the implementation will not be available (eg because we move into a new financial year or because they are required elsewhere).
- Does the effectiveness of this solution rely upon the actions of other people and
  – are they capable of carrying out what is required?
  – are they likely to meet our expectations?
  – are there any personal or political reasons why they may not behave as expected and required?
- Could a change in external factors throw us off course or prevent us carrying out certain parts of our plan? (eg National disputes, changes in social attitudes, government legislation, the environment or the economy.)

Sometimes it's necessary to draw up a rough plan for implementation before you can determine the potential risks involved (eg in terms of keeping to the time schedule). The process of planning for implementation is described in Chapter 11.

When you have identified areas of risk you need to calculate the probability of an undesirable outcome and the severity of its effects, eg there is a probability of 0.25 (25% chance) that our major competitor is more advanced in developing a similar service and, if this were true, it would mean that our intention of being first in the market will fail and make the solution unviable.

Some types of situation inevitably carry a substantial amount of risk, eg developing new technologies. If possible you should build into your solution ways of minimising risks, although ultimately you need to identify an acceptable level of risk for each risk factor.

If the risks associated with a particular solution are found to be unacceptable and inescapable it must be rejected and the next highest scoring solution evaluated for risks. This process continues until a totally acceptable solution is found.

Making the decision

When you make a decision you commit yourself to a particular course of action and take responsibility for its consequences. If you do not make this commitment you have not made a decision, so you can't proceed any further and you will not solve the problem.

Once you have decided upon a viable solution you may need to get approval to implement it. Even when this is not essential it's wise to seek the approval of the people affected and those who will be involved in implementation. Chapter 10 explains how to present your solution in the most effective way.

 # KEY POINTS

- The 'best' solution is often a compromise between conflicting needs and between the advantages and disadvantages of the various options.
- Solutions which don't meet the constraints of the situation must be rejected.
- The best of the remaining options is generally the one which fits the ideal solution most

closely, although you may use a different selection strategy.

- Before you accept a solution you must decide if any associated risks are acceptable.

PROJECT

Think about some of the recent situations in which you have needed to make a decision and answer yes or no to the following questions. If you have any doubts, answer no.

Did you decide first exactly what outcome would constitute an effective decision?

Did you identify the constraints of the situation?

Did you systematically evaluate all the options?

Did you make sure that you were aware of the risks involved before you made your final decision?

Did you make the decision and act upon it?

If you answered no to any of these questions it suggests that your decision making is not totally reliable. Using the methods described in this chapter should help you to improve your decision making technique. Make a note here of the *areas where you think you need to take more care over the way you evaluate different options.*

Chapter 10

Getting your solution accepted

Once you have decided on a solution to a particular problem *you may need to obtain other people's cooperation, approval or authority* in order to implement it successfully. With routine problems, where there is common understanding of what is involved, this is often straightforward and simply involves notifying the relevant people of your decision and how it will affect them. However, with complex and uncommon problems, and where major change or extensive use of resources is required, you should plan how to present your solution effectively. This chapter will help you to

- understand the reasons why people may oppose and possibly reject your solution
- prepare a presentation which optimises the chances of your solution being accepted
- deliver your presentation effectively.

The situations in which you need to 'sell' your solution to other people are listed in the previous chapter. If you have involved them in finding solutions and evaluating them you may already have gained their approval and commitment, although it will still be necessary to inform them of the details of your plan for implementing the solution. This plan forms part of your presentation of the solution for approval and is described in Chapter 11.

It can be frustrating to have to consult other people before you can implement a solution. In some situations this irritation is justified, such as when your manager has demanded consultation before you reorganise your workload, even though it doesn't affect other people. On other occasions it is in your own interests to consult others. Unless you get the agreement of those who have the authority to sanction your proposed actions you may be prevented from implementing the solution, and without the commitment of those involved in the implementation it may not be entirely successful.

Reasons for opposition to a solution

The manager of a small, dedicated research and development team in the packaging industry decided that it would be more productive if she coordinated individual efforts more closely. Unbeknown to the group, she spent 3 weeks devising a new management plan.

Instead of the team tackling problems by pooling their intellectual resources, she intended to give individuals a detailed brief on what areas she would like each of them to explore.

Ten minutes before the end of work on a Friday afternoon she called the team together. Handing out copies of her plan, she said: 'I've decided we can do a better job if each of you concentrates on one aspect of a particular problem. Read this over the weekend and give me your reaction on Monday.'

Irrespective of whether this new management plan was going to make the team more productive, this manager made some serious errors in trying to solve the problem of improving productivity, eg

- since it was likely to involve a change in working methods, she should have involved team members in looking for a solution
- the plan she gave to team members mentioned nothing about her reasons for believing there

was a problem, or how the new method of working would lead to greater productivity

- she decided to present her 'solution' at the end of the working week; this robbed individuals of the opportunity to discuss their concerns, which were likely to fester and create resentment before Monday arrived
- her manner of introducing the plan suggested a *fait accompli.*

However good a solution, the way it is introduced or presented to the people involved or affected can determine whether it will succeed or fail. The more opposition there is to your proposal the more likely it is to be rejected. Even if the people with the power to sanction the proposal are not opposed to it, opposition from others may influence their decision. Therefore it's important to try to recognise areas of potential opposition so that you can plan how to overcome them.

 ## ACTIVITY

List the reasons why people may oppose a solution you present to them.

GUIDELINES

There are many reasons why people may oppose a solution presented to them. Not all of these are related directly to the ideas and actions concerned. They include:

A poor solution
Any solution which does not deal with the problem effectively, or is impractical, or does not take into consideration all the relevant factors, should be opposed. If the solution does not fit the problem, or has unacceptable side-effects, you should not be proposing it.

Nature of the problem
When a problem is having serious consequences for the people listening to your proposal they will scrutinise it more closely than if the problem is having only minor effects. Similarly, if the people involved have a good knowledge of the problem or aspects of the solution it also will receive close scrutiny. Under these circumstances, any aspects of your solution which do not conform to the ideas or expectations of these people may be opposed simply because of differences of opinion.

Lack of interest in the problem can create opposition when people feel that you are wasting their time by involving them. Lack of knowledge of the problem area can also create opposition if you do not give people sufficient information to be able to understand your reasons for choosing that particular solution.

Individual needs and expectations
These can colour people's perceptions of, and reactions to, your proposed solution. For example, an individual who has a strong need to feel independent may oppose any solution which increases collective responsibility or encourages group working. Expectations of the outcome of solving a

particular problem can also create opposition. For example, a person with a grievance against the current method of grading because it places emphasis on qualifications rather than performance is likely to oppose any new grading system which does not increase the emphasis on performance.

Resistance to change

Some organisations and some managers are strongly resistant to change. In these situations a solution which involves considerable change in the status quo may meet strong opposition, even when it is good and presented well. Some organisations also do not have the structure or resources to accommodate major change and therefore senior management are likely to veto such solutions.

Mistrust of the solution

Many people have an in-built suspicion of solutions which are highly innovative, or yield high rewards by a simple method which seems 'too good to be true'.

Poor presentation

You can create opposition by not presenting your solution effectively, eg if you do not identify the benefits sufficiently to outweigh the disadvantages, not showing that you have considered side-effects and risks, giving inadequate information or not communicating it effectively so that people either misunderstand or are unable to evaluate the solution.

Poor timing

However sound the basic idea, an ill-timed solution can meet with opposition, eg proposing a solution which requires permanent additional manpower shortly after redundancies in another department; or suggesting a more centralised management structure when the current policy is to promote greater autonomy of company divisions.

Unsolicited ideas

If you have taken it upon yourself to solve a particular problem or exploit an opportunity and have not mentioned this to the people involved or affected, your solution will come as a complete surprise and could be received in a number of ways. They may be interested without having any intention of adopting your ideas; they may feel that you are interfering and perhaps even criticising them for the way they do things currently; or they may refuse to listen to your ideas. All of these responses are legitimate under the circumstances.

It is a waste of your time and could create antagonism if you try to force your ideas upon others. The only time it is worth presenting an unsolicited solution is when people have answered yes to a question like, 'I think I have found a way to ..., would you be interested in hearing more?'.

Interpersonal conflict

Your relationship with the people you are presenting your ideas to, and their perceptions of you, can have a profound effect on their reaction to your solution. These factors are very complex and often have been created over many years.

For example, a young, enthusiastic manager keen on applying the latest techniques may meet opposition from a more traditional, mature manager who resents the attempt to change things. Similarly, if, at some time in the distant past, you have criticised or rejected someone's ideas, when it is time to listen to your ideas they still may feel resentment and try to block them.

Getting a good solution accepted (you should *never try to sell a bad solution*) is a matter of persuasive communication and preparation is the key to success. This identifies the best way to communicate your solution.

Why may people oppose your solution?

To identify why your particular solution may be opposed you need to analyse two aspects of the situation:

- the problem and its solution
- the people involved and affected.

The problem and its solution

To present your solution persuasively you need to know how the people involved are likely to react to it, so that you can present it in such a way as to prevent opposition. The first step is to list the attributes of the problem and your solution which affect other people. The following questions will help you to explore some of the major factors:

- Who does the problem affect?
- What adverse effects are they experiencing?
- Which of these adverse effects does the solution remove?
- Does the solution call for major changes, and who will be affected most?
- Does the solution have adverse side-effects, and for whom?
- Is the solution unusual, and in what ways?
- Does its implementation require exceptional cooperation or action by any individuals, and how?

Answering these questions will help you to identify aspects of the solution which are likely to be of most interest to your audience. Some areas of possible opposition may be apparent already, eg if your solution does not deal with all the adverse effects of the problem, those people who will still be affected may oppose your solution.

The people involved and affected

To complete your identification of potential areas of opposition you need to ask yourself, *'how are people likely to react to this solution?'* This involves answering questions such as:

- Do any aspects of the problem or its solution have special significance for them? (eg Does it reflect badly on their previous performance or judgement; does it infringe on their area of operation or detract from their authority; does it compete with their needs for resources?)

- In what way will they want the situation to change when the problem is solved, and does the solution achieve this?
- Will they gain or lose with this solution, how and by how much?
- Will they want to achieve or gain something for themselves or others through this solution?
- Do they hold particularly strong views on any aspect of the problem or its solution? (eg Do they have an axe to grind?)
- Do they have stereotyped views? (eg Favouring the traditional approach.)

You are also one of the people involved, so you need to consider additional factors such as:

- What is their personal opinion of me? (eg Do any of them have reason to resent or mistrust you?)
- Are our views of the situation likely to coincide or differ, by how much, and in what ways?

By comparing your answers to all of these questions – about the problem, its solution and the people involved – you will be able to identify all the major sources of opposition. Assuming that your solution is timely, sound and deals with the problem effectively, *all of these possible causes of opposition can be avoided by the way you present your solution.*

Planning your presentation

Your solution may be presented verbally, on a one-to-one basis or in a meeting, or with a written report, depending on the situation. If there is more than one other person involved, and you have a choice, a meeting gives you the opportunity to get immediate feedback and respond persuasively to doubts and objections. However, most solutions which involve major changes or extensive use of resources are presented in reports. Whichever method you use, there are a number of tactics you can use to encourage acceptance and support of your solution.

ACTIVITY

List the ways in which you could encourage people to support a solution you propose.

GUIDELINES

Persuading people to accept your solution involves giving them reason to accept it rather than oppose it. This is achieved in a variety of ways:

Anticipate opposition

From analysing the problem, your solution and your audience, you should have a good idea of the opposition that could arise. Prepare responses to questions and objections that are likely to be raised. It's important that you explain the disadvantages as well as the advantages of your solution. If you try to disguise them it will give someone the opportunity to highlight them and create the impression that either you are not being truthful or have not considered the situation thoroughly. If your proposed solution involves major changes you should introduce these carefully, helping the people affected to accept and adjust to them.

Be prepared to listen to objections

Don't try to suppress objections. If you don't give people the opportunity to explain their objections you can create the impression that you are trying to 'gloss over' flaws in your solution and you deny yourself the opportunity to overcome the objections. Never argue with, or try to 'put down' someone who raises an objection. Your earlier analysis should have prepared you to overcome most objections.

Get them involved

Ideally, the best way to gain acceptance and commitment is to involve the relevant people in finding and evaluating solutions to the problem. However, even if you have not done this, there are still ways of getting them involved, eg:

- give them a role in the presentation, eg explaining how the solution affects their department

- give them a role in the implementation, either directly or in monitoring its effects
- allow them to contribute to your plan for implementation.

Get them interested

For people to accept and be fully committed to the successful implementation of your solution they must listen and fully understand the implications of the situation, particularly if they are involved in the implementation. The best way to ensure that they listen is to arouse their interest and one way of doing this is to tell them at the beginning of your presentation how they will benefit.

Demonstrate the importance of the problem

If you can show at the outset that the problem is important, either in its adverse effects or the benefits that could be gained, people are likely to be more interested in hearing how you intend to deal with the situation than if it was a relatively insignificant problem.

Appeal to their self-interest

Appealing to the needs and desires of individuals is a powerful way of gaining their acceptance, provided your solution does fulfil what you are offering. You should explain how people will benefit by your solution compared with the current situation. There is a wide range of motivating factors you can use, including recognition, security, power, pride, self-respect and reward. A new management structure, for example, could be sold on its more equitable sharing of power, or greater efficiency leading to a reduced workload and larger bonuses.

Justify the resources you want to use

Solutions which tie up resources over a long period of time are often rejected on this criterion alone. Acceptance is more likely if your solution uses resources over a limited period or in short bursts. The greater the resources required the more carefully you need to explain the reasons for using them ie. the benefits to be gained. You must show your solution to be cost-effective, ideally by giving hard facts about the return on investment.

Explain your solution effectively

The key to a successful presentation lies in the way you explain your solution. You must make it easy to understand, show that it has been well thought out and that it's the best solution available under the circumstances.

Show enthusiasm for your solution

This can be infectious. If you don't show enthusiasm for your solution neither will others.

Be flexible

Be prepared to vary your plan to accommodate individual needs, particularly those of people who are required to take action or provide resources for implementing the solution.

Be prepared to make concessions

One way of encouraging acceptance of a solution is to give way on certain points. This is particularly important where people expect negotiation or bargaining, such as issues concerning union members. To prepare yourself for this bargaining, identify the aspects of your proposal which are not essential to achieving your objective. You can trade these for others which are essential to the success of your solution.

Choose the right moment for your presentation

If you have a choice, make your presentation at a time when your audience will be least distracted by thoughts of other things (eg not just before lunch or at the end of the day), and when they will have time to consider your proposition fully before major interruptions (eg not just before a weekend or holiday).

The final step is to combine all this information into an effective presentation.

Making your presentation

The way you present your information is crucial to success, whether it's done verbally or in a report. In general you should aim to make your presentation clear, simple and to the point. To help explain your solution in a way that people will understand easily, follow these guidelines:

- keep it short and simple – don't confuse them with too much data or a very complex argument – but make sure that you cover all the important factors
- avoid ambiguities
- prepare your presentation according to your audience's level of knowledge and understanding of the topics covered
- avoid any words or terms people may not understand, eg jargon and technical terms.

With complex issues you should concentrate on the major advantages and disadvantages, leaving the others for discussion later, if necessary, or inclusion in an appendix to your report. You should state at the beginning of your presentation that this is what you intend to do. Most important of all, your presentation should be a logical progression from the facts of the current situation to how your proposed solution will deal with the problem effectively.

Verbal presentations

With verbal presentations the order in which you present your ideas is particularly important. If you reveal your solution at the outset, for example, people may foresee disadvantages and raise an objection before you have explained how you intend to handle the situation. This can lead to confusion and early on people may get the impression that the solution is impractical. *First impressions are difficult to change.*

The best way to avoid this type of situation is to follow these steps, *checking that your audience agree at each stage* before moving on:

- state the overall objective in solving the problem
- describe the constraints on the situation
- briefly describe all the results that you felt were required and their relative importance
- briefly state all the options you considered without saying which you have chosen
- describe the criteria of evaluation you have used and their relative importance
- state which option you have chosen, explaining how it is the best solution available and the associated risks that you have identified
- explain how the solution will be implemented
- state how the results will be identified and measured.

This strategy uses the same methodical approach that you used in constructing the solution, making it easier to explain clearly and to deal with objections step-by-step.

Many people get very anxious about making verbal presentations. Thorough preparation and rehearsal will help you to overcome this fear and to ensure that you convey your ideas effectively. Factors such as overt signs of nervousness and continual hesitation can convey uncertainty about your solution or that you are trying to hide something. Following these guidelines will help you to create the right impression:

- use unobtrusive key-word notes if you cannot remember all you want to say
- use visual aids if they help to get your ideas across more effectively
- speak confidently
- project your energy and enthusiasm through your voice (lively, but not over-effusive), posture (upright and relaxed) and gestures (natural)

- watch your audience for signs of how they are reacting to what you say (eg confused, impatient, unattentive) and respond accordingly
- answer questions carefully and succinctly (your preparation should have uncovered most of the likely questions).

Making effective verbal presentations is a skill which requires practice. Rehearsal, preferably with an audience which can comment on your performance, will help you to perfect a specific presentation.

Written presentations

Reports can vary from a simple one-page outline to a large bound volume of 100 pages or more, but they should never contain unnecessary information. The features of a good report can be grouped under four headings.

Contents

A written report can be perused at will and digested at the reader's own pace. There is a temptation, therefore, not to worry about keeping the report short and simple. However, the easier you make it for people, the more likely they are to read and accept what you have to say. Interest will be sustained if you get to the point quickly.

Structure

The structure of a report should help people to understand your proposal. This means following the guidelines given for verbal presentations, presenting information in a logical, step-by-step fashion. With complex issues only the main points should be covered in the body of the report, with supporting evidence and the less significant information given in appendices. If the body of the report is more than about ten pages, it may be desirable to give an abstract at the beginning covering the essential points, eg the problem, its effects, and the recommended solution.

Style

The writing style you use should make the contents easy to read and understand. All the factors relating to jargon and so on, mentioned for verbal presentations, also apply to reports. Sentences and paragraphs should be short and written in a conversational style unless the subject or application demands otherwise.

Layout

The layout of words on the page should give the appearance of being easy to follow and understand. Don't crowd pages, leave wide margins, give clear headings and emphasise important points.

Writing reports effectively is a skill that can be developed with practice. A good book on the subject will help you to use reports effectively.

What to do if your solution is rejected

It is not uncommon for ideas to be rejected, particularly when they involve major changes, are innovative, or require extensive use of resources. If your idea is rejected you have a number of options:

- first check that you presented your idea effectively; if not, it may be worth re-presenting it if you have the opportunity
- consider whether you can present the idea to someone else with the appropriate authority to sanction it, or who could bring pressure to bear on the decision makers, eg those who will benefit most from your solution
- improve your solution to overcome the objections, and re-present it
- look for another solution, bearing in mind the reasons your first solution was rejected.

Trying to get your solution accepted can be frustrating and difficult, particularly in situations where you are encroaching on other people's territory or where there is no existing yardstick to measure the likely outcome. If it's an idea that you believe in, perseverance often pays off.

KEY
POINTS

- It may be necessary to obtain other people's approval and cooperation to implement your solution successfully.
- Carefully planning how to present your solution will improve your chances of gaining acceptance and cooperation.
- There are a variety of persuasive tactics you can use to influence your audience.

PROJECT

When next you need the agreement or cooperation of other people try using some of the methods described in this chapter. Afterwards, think about the effects they had and how you could apply them more effectively.

Chapter 11

Implementing your solution

Implementation is the culmination of all your work in solving a problem and requires careful attention to detail. There are three basic stages involved:

- planning and preparing to implement the solution
- implementing and monitoring the action
- reviewing and analysing the success of the action.

Planning and preparation

Planning and preparation is the key to successful implementation. The more important the problem, or the more complex the actions required to solve it, the more thorough your planning and preparation needs to be to ensure success.

ACTIVITY

Imagine that you are planning and preparing to implement a solution. Briefly describe what you would need to do before you could achieve the following things.

To be able to

I would need to ...

Inform people of precisely what is required of them

Coordinate the various actions required to solve the problem

Arrange for the necessary resources to be available

Ensure that people carry out what is required of them effectively

GUIDELINES

These questions highlight the main features of planning and preparation, which involve:

- constructing a plan of action
  1. the actions required
  2. scheduling the actions
  3. the resources required
  4. measures to counter adverse consequences
  5. management of the action
  6. reviewing the plan
- selecting, briefing and training those involved.

Constructing a plan of action

Basically, *the plan of action describes what actions are required and how they will be implemented to ensure success.* Unless the problem is simple or routine, you need to construct a detailed plan of action. This involves systematically identifying and recording the following elements:

1. The actions required

These must be identified fully and precisely, otherwise the results expected will not be achieved. The expected effects of these actions must also be identified, so that you will know when they have been carried out successfully. This part of the plan can be constructed as follows:

- state your objective
- list the individual goals in the order in which they must be achieved to reach that objective
- identify what actions are required to achieve each goal, determine the sequence in which they need to be carried out, and record them alongside each goal

- define, in measurable terms, what a successful outcome will be for each action and add the details to the plan.

The sequence you choose for the various actions and goals is determined by a number of factors. In some situations it may be necessary to complete one action or set of actions before another can begin, eg laying a foundation before building a wall. Actions also have to run consecutively when they each use the same resource to its available capacity. On other occasions actions can run concurrently, such as when each member of a team is assigned a specific piece of equipment to test and evaluate.

With all but the very simplest plans it's wise to *use a diagram to represent the sequence of actions* and how they contribute to the overall objective. This helps to show how the actions interact and to reveal areas of possible conflict. Actions should be fitted together as closely as possible, to prevent wastage of resources, while allowing some margin for overrun. To do this you need to prepare a time schedule for the actions.

2. Scheduling the actions

To create *a time schedule* for the actions, first you identify the time required to complete each action. By representing this information on the diagram you can calculate at what stage, relative to the starting time, each action will commence and finish, and determine the total time required to achieve the objective. Simple plans can be represented by a chart which uses bars to show the sequence and duration of the actions. (See Figure 11.1.)

More complex plans require a more flexible structure, like a chain diagram or flow chart (see Chapter 7). Diagrams help you to arrange the actions in a way which makes the best use of time and other resources. For example, if two actions each require two days' use of an excavator which can be hired only on a weekly basis, ideally these actions should be scheduled for the same week. When completed, the diagram also shows which of the actions it is most crucial to complete

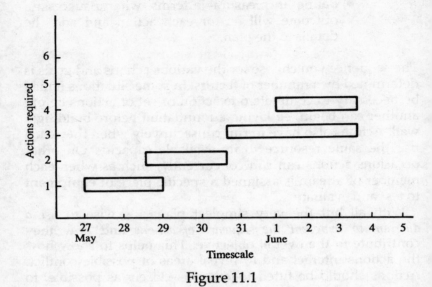

Figure 11.1

on time (eg draining a flooded site before the excavators move in), and how a delay or time-saving in completing one action will affect all the others (eg bad weather may delay the commencement of one action and have a knock-on effect).

In drawing up a schedule it's important not to be over-optimistic in the time you allow for each action. Additional time is required to accommodate delays and unforeseen obstacles, particularly with actions which must be completed on time or which are susceptible to delays. Methods for identifying potential delays are described in Section 4 below.

3. The resources required

For each action the resources required have to be precisely defined along a number of parameters, including the type, amount and when they are required. Each resource is considered individually:

Time is sometimes overlooked but it can be a key resource in some situations, eg completing the installation of new manufacturing plant before the end of the annual 'shutdown' period. It can be defined by answering these questions

- What time is available before the deadline for achieving each action/goal/the overall objective?
- Are these timings compatible?
- Whose time is required?
- Will this time be spent within normal working hours?

Manpower may come from within and outside the organisation and can be defined by answering the questions

- How many people will be required?
- What skills, qualities and knowledge will they need to carry out the actions required of them?
- When and where will they be required?
- Will they be available when and where required?
- Will they be available for the length of time required?
- What briefing and training will they need to be able to carry out their tasks effectively?

Money can be defined by answering the questions

- How much will be needed?
- In what form? (eg cash, cheque, foreign currency)
- How will it be acquired? (eg loan, grant, endowment)
- What will be the source? (eg profits, merchant bank, local or central government)
- How will it be used and is this compatible with the source? (eg if it's a development grant does the plan use it appropriately?)
- When and where will it be required?
- Will it be available when and where required?
- Does it need to be repaid, and when?

- Will it be recouped, how, and when? (eg through increased profits)
- Will there be additional cost in using this money? (eg interest or handling charges)
- Have the costs of all other resources been included?

Materials may fall into a number of categories, including consumables, raw materials, and equipment (for temporary or permanent use). They can be defined by answering the questions

- What type of materials will be required?
- If capital equipment is required, how will it be financed? (eg lease, loan)
- What are the specifications of the materials required? (eg quality, size)
- What wastage is likely to occur?
- In what quantities are they required?
- When and where will they be required?
- Will they be available when and where required?
- Will transport be required?
- What handling (human and mechanical) will be required?
- Will storage space be required, where, how much, for how long, and will it be available?

Space can be defined by answering the questions

- What space will be required?
- How much space will be required?
- Where will the space be required?
- Does it have to be of a particular type (eg covered, with amenities) or with particular dimensions?
- How long will the space be required?

Information may form a part of the manpower resource (eg expert advice or skills) but it can also be a resource in its own right (eg renting a mailing list for a direct mail campaign). To define this resource you need to answer the questions

- What specific information will be required?
- Is this information available from within the organisation or does it have to be bought-in?
- Where specifically is it available?
- When and where will it be required?
- Will it be available when and where required?
- How long will it be required?

When you are calculating the resources required to implement a solution it's vital not to under-estimate. A shortage could disrupt implementation completely and possibly incur heavy penalties, eg having to pay a consultant for doing nothing while he's waiting for the installation of a piece of equipment. Sometimes you may have to adapt your plan of action to suit the availability of resources.

Once you have made a complete list of the resource requirements, *draw up a schedule of resources*, showing how and when they will be requested, from whom, and when and where they are to be delivered. It's important to allow sufficient time between ordering and the required delivery date to ensure that any delay will not disrupt your time schedule.

4. Measures to counter adverse consequences

These have to be included in the plan. Although you have considered the areas of risk and possible side-effects when constructing and evaluating your solution, and adapted it to try to minimise the adverse consequences, you need to identify everything that could go wrong during implementation and devise countermeasures. This includes even minor problems, such as a temporary power cut which prevents the use of equipment.

The steps involved are similar to those used to evaluate and minimise the risks associated with the solution, only more detailed.

ACTIVITY

Name three areas in which it is most likely that something will go wrong during implementation and briefly describe how you should augment your plan to take account of this possibility.

1.

2.

3.

These possibilities can be accommodated in the plan by ...

GUIDELINES

There are certain features of a plan of action which can make it more susceptible to something going wrong. To identify these and make provision in your plan to deal with them, you should examine your plan step-by-step and follow these stages:

- *identify everything that could go wrong;* look for areas where, for example,
  - timing is crucial (eg with delays, could a deadline be missed?)
  - a slippage in timing could bring subsequent actions into conflict (eg so that they simultaneously require the same resource)
  - two or more activities coincide (eg will they interfere with each other?)
  - there is no way of predicting what may happen (eg because of lack of knowledge or experience)
  - there is heavy reliance on facilities or equipment (eg could they fail?)
  - there is heavy reliance on the cooperation and efforts of people (eg will they perform as required?)
  - all available resources in a particular category are being used (eg could an unexpected event require their more urgent use elsewhere?)
  - external factors could affect the actions required (eg withdrawal of labour in a national dispute) or the effectiveness of the results (eg a change in market needs)
- *analyse and evaluate the consequences,* eg
  - what are the effects if this happens?
  - how serious are they?
  - what is their relative seriousness?

- what is the probability of them happening (low, medium or high)?
- *define how you could recognise trouble* as early as possible, eg through the detection of unexpected changes in predicted events
- *devise countermeasures* where possible, either to prevent the cause of trouble or minimise its effects
- *incorporate* the method of recognition and the appropriate countermeasure into your plan.

Adverse consequences which have the highest probability of occurring combined with the greatest seriousness should be tackled first and every effort made to ensure that provision is made in your plan to counter them effectively. Even if time is short and it requires extensive work, you can only afford to omit minor adverse consequences with a low probability of occurrence. Although problems may not arise during implementation, if they do your plan must contain appropriate countermeasures which can be taken without jeopardising the rest of the plan.

5. Management of the action

Unless the solution is very simple or routine you must specify how the implementation will be monitored and controlled. This enables the manpower to be appropriately led and managed, their progress to be measured at specific intervals, and appropriate action to be taken to correct any variance from the plan. The following steps help to identify how to manage the implementation:

- identify actions which require on-the-job supervision and monitoring (eg where individuals have no previous experience of the actions required of them)
- identify the stages at which progress should be measured (eg upon completion of individual goals or major activities; at critical phases)

- specify exactly what results are expected to have been achieved at these stages
- specify how and by whom the actual results will be measured
- ensure that appropriate measures to correct any variance between the expected and the actual results are specified in the plan.

The stages you identify for measuring progress are, in effect, *deadlines for achieving specific results*. These must be stated as a specific time or date in the overall time schedule. Unspecific or woolly deadlines make implementation difficult to manage and can lead to disaster. The frequency of measuring progress is dependent upon a number of factors:

- what is practical (eg economical and not interfering significantly with progress)
- the rate at which the situation is likely to change (eg major building works compared with delicate negotiations over a couple of days)
- the seriousness of potential variances from the plan (eg points at which unnoticed mistakes in the construction of a distillation plant could make its operation dangerous).

Provision should also be made to monitor the solution once it has been implemented, so that any unforeseen adverse consequences arising in the long term can be detected. For example, has a change in the system created a bottleneck in processing work, or resulted in undue pressure on one individual or department?

6. Reviewing the plan
Finally, you need to check the plan to ensure that

- the actions listed will achieve the various goals and the overall objective
- your time schedule is workable and can accommodate unexpected delays

- your estimation of resources is accurate
- the plan for managing the action will enable it to be kept on course.

Drawing up a plan of action is the most crucial stage in ensuring efficient implementation and it must be accurate and thorough. This plan provides a blueprint for the remaining stages of implementation.

Selecting, briefing and training those involved

Your plan of action provides most of the information you require at this stage.

ACTIVITY

Imagine you have an important task to do which is outside the scope of your department's usual work and you have to delegate it to someone else. Briefly describe the steps you will go through to ensure that the task is completed efficiently.

GUIDELINES

This situation is very similar to having to get your solution implemented successfully. You need to go through the following stages:

- select individuals with the appropriate skills, qualities and knowledge required to carry out the various actions effectively
- brief these people so that they know and understand what they are required to do
- give training, if necessary, to individuals who do not meet the exact requirements for carrying out their assigned tasks effectively.

Selection involves comparing the skills, qualities and knowledge required for specific tasks with those available amongst individual members of the workforce. By identifying the ideal attributes for carrying out each action effectively – both what is required and what is to be avoided – you can construct a model of the ideal candidate. Selection then consists of finding the best match to this ideal amongst members of the workforce.

Once you have selected appropriate individuals you need to draw up a list of what actions each is required to carry out, the results they will be expected to achieve, and what responsibilities they have for achieving these results.

Frequently there will be at least some aspects of your plan for which the individuals available are not ideally suited. If the discrepancy is large it may be necessary to buy in manpower with the appropriate attributes. However, frequently the shortfall can be overcome by careful briefing or specific training.

Briefing is often the final step before a plan is implemented. As in any other type of communication, it must be planned and executed carefully to ensure that it's effective. The following steps will help you to brief people effectively:

- give individuals reasonable advance warning of what will be required of them
- prepare your briefing carefully so that it is clear, comprehensive and can be understood easily by everyone involved (the guidelines in Chapter 10 will help you)
- after the briefing, check that everyone has understood what they are required to do by asking them to repeat your instructions.

Your instructions should *state clearly the responsibilities of each individual and the scope of their authority in carrying out their task.* It's important to give a level of authority which enables individuals to use their initiative and not be bound rigidly to the plan. For example, if they foresee a problem arising they need the freedom to act immediately if necessary.

The *way* you communicate your message is very important. Some individuals may have a different view of the situation and different attitudes to your own, particularly if they have not been involved in finding and evaluating solutions. The guidelines in Chapter 10 will help you to encourage their cooperation and commitment to carry out their tasks effectively.

Training can be expensive and time-consuming. If people with the appropriate skills are not readily available you need to compare the advantages and disadvantages of training them or buying-in the necessary skills, eg training may provide individuals with skills which are of value in other aspects of their work; hiring a consultant may create a valuable business contact.

Once people have been briefed on what they are required to do and other appropriate resources have been arranged, the plan of action can be implemented.

Implementing and monitoring the action

Once action has been initiated, it has to be supervised and monitored to ensure that the plan is followed accurately, implementing corrective action when necessary. The details of this stage are specified in the plan of action.

Supervising the action ensures that individuals carry out their tasks efficiently according to the plan.

Monitoring progress enables you to identify whether or not the results being achieved are meeting the planned requirements, and if not, why not. A decision can then be made on the action required to put the plan back on course. Reviewing the overall achievement once the plan has progressed significantly will indicate how well it is achieving the objective. If there are major discrepancies it suggests that the plan is inadequate and needs to be revised.

Taking corrective action may involve implementing the appropriate countermeasure laid down in the plan, or taking unplanned action to counter unforeseen problems. For example, if time has been lost in completing one activity, other activities may have to be completed more quickly than planned in order to meet a deadline. Minor problems which are unlikely to recur may not require any action. Major faults in the plan may make it necessary to abandon implementation if no appropriate corrective action is possible.

These three processes must be maintained until the plan is completed.

Reviewing and analysing the outcome

When the plan has been completed and the solution implemented it is important to measure and analyse its success. This tells you whether the solution has been effective in solving the problem and how useful it will be in solving similar problems in the future. There are three stages involved:

- measure the success of the solution by comparing the outcome of the action with the expected results
- analyse any discrepancy to identify the reasons for it
- take further action if necessary.

Measuring success

Right at the start of solving the problem you identified the objective you wanted to achieve and stated it in measurable terms. Now you need to compare the results you have achieved with those you set out to achieve and note any discrepancies. In some situations it may be necessary to measure the results regularly over a period of time to check whether the initial results are being maintained, eg when the novelty of a new system has worn off, you need to know if people are still using it efficiently. Changes in the effectiveness of the solution also can occur with changes in the objective, eg in a fast moving market a 'new' product doesn't remain new for long.

Analysing discrepancies

This helps you to identify how and why you have either exceeded or failed to achieve the results you wanted. This helps you to identify where you can take further action to overcome a shortfall in the results. It also helps you to identify the strengths and weaknesses of your approach to solving the problem – knowledge which is essential in improving your problem solving skills.

Taking further action

This may be required for a number of reasons, eg when the initial results are inadequate, when the results are not maintained without intervention, and when the results do not meet a new objective which has arisen. To decide what further action is required you need to define new objectives and any associated obstacles – a new problem for you to solve and *the process has come full circle*.

Implementation reveals the fruits of your labour in

ding the problem. If you get the results that you wanted you can congratulate yourself on a job well done, although there is always room for improvement. If your solution isn't as successful as you had hoped, it's an ideal opportunity to improve your problem solving skills by finding out why.

KEY
POINTS

- The more important the problem, or the more complex the actions required to solve it, the more planning and preparation you need to do.
- Action must be monitored to ensure that it is being carried out effectively and having the desired effects; if not, corrective action must be taken.
- Once the action is completed, the outcome must be measured to check that it has provided an effective solution; if not, further action may be required.

PROJECT

List some of the specific areas of your work where you may benefit from applying the following principles described in this chapter:

1. Drawing up a plan before taking action.

2. Briefing staff on what is required of them.

3. Monitoring work in progress.

4. Reviewing the success of particular actions.

Chapter 12

Your ACTION PLAN
for solving problems

We all possess the thinking skills required to solve problems but learning when and how to apply them most effectively requires practice. There are many steps and processes involved and to find effective solutions you need to follow them methodically. The experienced problem solver does this automatically, knowing exactly what is required at each stage. Until you can do the same, this chapter will help you to build a checklist summarising all the steps you need to follow.

 ACTIVITY

This will help you to recall and summarise the topics covered in this book. Treat it as the first step in learning to follow the necessary steps automatically. Allow yourself about 45 minutes and answer the following questions in note form. If you get stuck, refer to the relevant chapter.

Briefly describe how you can ensure that 'blocks' do not hinder your problem solving. (Chapter 3)

List the situations in which it's best to solve a problem in a group. (Chapter 8)

List the main things you need to do to recognise and define problems effectively. (Chapter 5)

How do you decide when it is best to take action over a problem, or if it is necessary to take action at all? (Chapter 5)

List the cycle of stages involved in finding possible solutions to a problem. (Chapter 6)

Briefly describe what you need to do to decide which of the possible solutions will be most effective in solving a problem. (Chapter 9)

Imagine you need the sanction of others before you can implement a particular solution. List five steps you would take to maximise the chances of it being accepted. (Chapter 10)

List the main steps required to ensure that a solution is implemented successfully. (Chapter 11)

GUIDELINES

The following **Action Plan** covers the main features of the problem solving process. You can use it as a guide in tackling the problems you encounter. Remember that these stages often mix and overlap. You may have noted additional points which are relevant to your particular work situation. There are spaces in each section for you to make a note of these.

Recognising and overcoming problem solving blocks

There is a large range of blocks which can hinder your problem solving. To avoid their effects you need to

- be constantly aware of the factors which can hinder problem solving
- learn specific techniques for overcoming different types of block
- apply these techniques when you recognise that a block is hindering your problem solving.

Notes:

Involving others in solving the problem

Some problems are solved more effectively in a group. The more times you answer 'yes' to the following questions, the more appropriate it is to tackle the problem as a group:

- Can the problem be defined in many different ways?
- Is information from many different sources required?
- Is it a very specialised problem?
- Does the problem have implications for many people?
- Are there likely to be many possible solutions?
- Is it a complex problem with many different aspects?
- Will a solution need to be agreed by others?

The deciding question will always be: 'Are suitable and relevant people available to work together in solving this problem?' There are a number of techniques designed specifically for solving problems as a group, including brainstorming and Synectics.

Notes:

Recognising and defining the problem

This is a key stage in solving problems effectively.
To **recognise problems efficiently** you need to

- be aware of the areas in which problems may arise
- establish specific methods of detection
  - monitor performance against agreed standards
  - observe staff to detect behaviour which may reflect an underlying problem
  - listen to staff so that you are aware of their concerns
  - regularly review and compare current and past performance and behaviour to detect gradual deterioration.

To **define problems effectively** you need to distinguish between open-ended and closed problems and analyse them differently.

Closed problems:

- identify and record all aspects of the deviation from the norm (the Kepner–Tregoe approach is a good method)
- analyse the information to identify possible causes
- identify the real cause
- define in a similar way to open-ended problems.

Open-ended problems

- identify all the possible objectives that you may want to achieve – in terms of 'How to ...?'
- select the 'How to ...?' statements which most accurately represent your problem
- for each one, list the characteristics of the current and desired situations
- add details of any obstacles which may prevent you achieving the desired situation

- add details of the needs of other people who are affected.

Notes:

Deciding if and when to act

Not all problems are important enough to merit the resources required to solve them. Even when they do, it's sometimes better to wait rather than to act immediately. Answering the following questions will tell you if the problem requires action and whether it would be best to act now or wait.

- Will the problem solve itself?
- Are the effects significant enough to merit the resources that may be required to solve the problem?
- Is the problem diminishing? (wait)
- Are the obstacles diminishing? (wait)
- Will the cause subside? (wait)
- Is the problem having serious effects? (act)
- Is the problem growing? (act)
- Are the obstacles growing? (act)
- Is there a deadline? (act)

Notes:

Finding possible solutions

Open-ended problems usually have many possible solutions, while closed problems have one or a limited number of ways to overcome the cause. To find possible solutions you need to follow these stages, which form a cycle:

Identify the relevant information
Initially based on your problem definition:
- What information is needed?
- Why is it needed?
- Where can it be obtained?
- How reliable will it be?
- How can it be obtained?

Collect and record the information
This is a systematic process, starting with the information which will take the longest time to collect. Checking the accuracy of the information is vital.

Represent the information
Create a model of the problem. This helps to give it structure and helps in your search for solutions. At this stage it may be necessary to look for other possible causes of closed problems.

Define criteria of effectiveness

This gives direction to your search for solutions and involves listing the characteristics of an 'ideal' solution:

- What benefits are you seeking?
- What obstacles/causes have to be dealt with?
- What are the constraints on the situation?
- What will be acceptable to those involved or affected?
- What level of risk is acceptable?

Some of these factors can only be defined once you have found possible solutions.

Construct courses of action to solve the problem

This involves finding ways of achieving the criteria of effectiveness you have defined. There are five sources of ideas:

- past experience of similar situations
- logical deduction from the facts
- other people
- published sources
- creative idea generation techniques.

The possible solutions are modified and refined to take account of factors which could influence their effectiveness, eg

- What could go wrong?
- Are there factors over which you have no control?
- Could the objectives change?
- Could the obstacles become more intractable?
- Could new obstacles arise?
- Could this solution create an opportunity that can be exploited at the same time?

Notes:

Evaluating your solutions

Deciding which of the possible solutions will be most effective in solving the problem is a systematic process which can be divided into stages:

Involve others
- when you have a formal obligation to consult them
- when you require additional information to help in the evaluation
- when you require their expert skills
- when you need their commitment.

Define the 'ideal' solution:
- results required
  - benefits in terms of the objective
  - dealing effectively with obstacles/causes
  - acceptance of the solution by other people
- constraints
  - limits of resources
  - minimum results acceptable
  - maximum disadvantages that can be tolerated.

The results required are given numerical values according to their relative importance. Where the outcome is uncertain you need to calculate probabilities.

Eliminate unviable solutions, ie those which do not meet the constraints.

Evaluate the remaining solutions, ie estimate how well each one fits the ideal solution. The ideal fit on each dimension of the results required is given an arbitrary value. Disadvantages are given a negative value. Solutions are evaluated by multiplying the relative fit by the relative value of each result. The best solution is the one with the highest aggregate score.

Assess the risks associated with this solution, eg

- Is the information used in the construction and evaluation of the solution accurate?
- If not, could this put the success of the solution in jeopardy, and how?
- What could happen if the implementation does not go as planned?
- What are the chances of these things happening?
- What would be the effects?
- How severe would they be?

If the risks are unacceptable and cannot be reduced sufficiently by adapting the solution it must be rejected and the next highest scoring solution assessed for risks. Continue this process until you find an acceptable solution.

Make the decision to implement the solution. Until you commit yourself to taking action you cannot proceed any further and the problem will remain unsolved.

Notes:

Getting your solution accepted

To encourage people to accept your solution, and to gain their commitment to its successful implementation, first you need to draw up a plan for implementing the solution (see the next section) and then to

Identify areas of possible opposition by considering

- how the solution could adversely affect the people involved
- what they expect or need from the solution and what it will give them
- their feelings about the nature of the problem and your solution
- their relationship with, and perception of, you
- what the solution requires of them.

Prepare a presentation which optimises the chances of your solution being accepted and supported, eg

- incorporate measures to counter opposition
- get people involved and interested
- appeal to their self-interest
- justify your proposed use of resources
- explain your solution effectively
- be prepared to make concessions.

Deliver your presentation effectively, whether in a meeting or a report, eg

- choose the right moment
- make it clear and easy to understand
- show your enthusiasm for the solution.

Persevere until you succeed, either by improving your presentation or your solution, presenting it to someone else, or by looking for a different solution.

Notes:

Implementing your solution

To ensure that your solution is implemented successfully, and achieves the results you expect, you need to

Plan and prepare to implement the solution:

- draw up a plan of action
  - the actions required
  - a schedule of actions
  - the resources required (what and when)
  - measures to counter adverse consequences
  - management of the action
- review the plan to ensure that it is adequate and accurate
- select, brief and train those involved to ensure that they have the appropriate information, skills and qualities required to implement the action successfully.

Implement and monitor the action:

- supervise the action
- monitor its implementation and effects

- keep it on track by countering unexpected delays, faults and obstacles.

Review and analyse the success of the action:

- compare the outcome of the action with the expected results
- identify any discrepancies (positive or negative) and analyse them to identify the causes
- take further action if necessary eg to correct a shortfall or to maintain current results.

Notes:

Where to next?

Although you may have learnt a great deal about the process of problem solving from this book and had some practice in applying the various techniques, *the only way to ensure that you always find the best available solution to a problem is through continuous practice.*

HOW TO BECOME A BETTER PROBLEM SOL

- have confidence in your ability to learn
- practise being methodical and using the appropriate techniques
- be patient with your progress
- analyse your mistakes and learn from them
- if your working environment is not conducive to effective problem solving, either try to change it or learn how to avoid its effects
- don't be afraid to ask for help in the form of advice or training

KEY
POINTS

Improving your problem solving skills requires

- a methodical approach
- continuous practice
- perseverance
- confidence in being able to succeed.

PROJECT

Select a problem with a high priority which you are facing currently and use the Action Plan in this chapter to help you find an effective solution. Refer to previous chapters if you need additional guidance.

Index